THE RHYTHM
OF
ENGLISH PROSE

T0382066

THE RHYTHM
OF
ENGLISH PROSE

A Manual for Students

BY

NORTON R. TEMPEST
Sometime William Noble Fellow in the
University of Liverpool

CAMBRIDGE
AT THE UNIVERSITY PRESS
1930

CAMBRIDGE
UNIVERSITY PRESS

University Printing House, Cambridge CB2 8BS, United Kingdom

Published in the United States of America by Cambridge University Press, New York

Cambridge University Press is part of the University of Cambridge.

It furthers the University's mission by disseminating knowledge in the pursuit of
education, learning and research at the highest international levels of excellence.

www.cambridge.org
Information on this title: www.cambridge.org/9781107649828

© Cambridge University Press 1930

First published 1930
First paperback edition 2014

A catalogue record for this publication is available from the British Library

ISBN 978-1-107-64982-8 Paperback

To

MY MOTHER AND FATHER

PREFACE

THIS work is primarily intended for the use of those who are approaching the subject of English prose-rhythm for the first time. It has been the writer's aim throughout to avoid controversy, and to present, in a simple way, a subject which readily lends itself to confusion. He has no desire to impose his views upon his reader, but would afford the opportunity of making a beginning, whence any special direction that may seem attractive may be followed. In the matter of scansion there is no intention to dogmatise. Syllables and groups frequently occur whose stress is uncertain, but this does not change the general principles and features with which this book is chiefly concerned. Finally, readers are reminded that this is a pioneer work, the first of its kind in English, and thus, unlike text-books on better known subjects, cannot benefit from the errors of its predecessors. If it will stimulate others to follow, and help them to go further, whilst serving in the meantime as a guide, it will achieve its purpose.

The writer wishes to record his gratitude to the authors of the books listed in the Bibliography, and, in particular, to Professor Oliver Elton, with whose guidance and encouragement he first embarked on research in prose-rhythm; to the founder and trustees of the William Noble Fellowship Fund, through whose generosity he has found time for its pursuit; and to Professor L. C. Martin who has, by his unfailing kindness and assistance, placed him under a debt which he cannot repay.

N. R. T.

January 1930

CONTENTS

CHAPTER I

RHYTHM

IT is, perhaps, unfortunate, but, in the present circumstances, inevitable, that any attempt to discuss the rhythm of prose should be unsatisfactory unless preceded by an inquiry into the nature of rhythm in general and of auditory rhythm in particular. There has been much recent speculation on the subject of rhythm, but in spite of this its nature still remains controversial and undefined.

Most, if not all, human beings show a tendency, more or less developed in different individuals, to organise any series of impressions into something like order, and pleasure is obtained during the satisfaction of this tendency. Pleasure arises in the course of satisfying this impulse or tendency; it is not, or should not be, the end in itself. Discussion of this must, however, be left to the psychologists, as it can have no place here. It is sufficient for the present purpose to show that pleasure in such movements as can be organised in an orderly way is natural to man, although the capacity for such organisation is much greater in some men than in others. There is also a difference in material; phenomena, such as music, which possess ordered movement, will obviously offer less difficulty to the satisfaction of the tendency to order impressions than more irregular material.

Proof of the tendency to organise impressions in a regular manner, and of the pleasure obtained during its satisfaction, is everywhere about us. It is well known that manual work, especially, is much easier to do regularly than in haphazard jerks. The road-mender wields his mallet, and the blacksmith strikes the iron, at measured intervals. When hurdling, the athlete, by taking the same number of steps between the hurdles and springing from the same foot each time, jumps regularly, finding that this is much easier than taking the hurdles haphazard. The same is true of most work. The more ordered the execution, the less tiring it becomes. Sailors sing over their tasks, and how many soldiers prefer to march without a band? Experiments are being made at the present time to discover how manual work may be made easier by the provision of a musical accompaniment.

The manifestations of *rhythm*, the name commonly associated with the tendency to organise impressions in this way, are found in the earliest ages of history and in the most primitive conditions. Thus there are savage tribes whose sense of rhythm, as shown in their dances, is very highly developed. We are told that they can bring even the most apparently irregular impressions into an orderly sequence or system, carrying out, for instance, the most elaborate schemes of syncopation. Mr W. M. Patterson suggests that in this respect they are our superiors. "Modern sophistication has inhibited many native instincts, and the mere fact that our con-

ventional dignity usually forbids us to sway our bodies
or to tap our feet when we hear effective music has
deprived us of unexpected pleasures. Certain it is that
the faculty of the American Indian in the execution of
syncopating rhythms is matched in most of us by a
thoroughly blunted process characterised by hesitation
and awkwardness".[1] Longinus writes that a Greek
audience would often beat time with the speaker; "he
shows us how acute and well-trained the ears of a Greek
must have been by saying that the audience of such a
style sometimes actually beat time like dancers with
the speaker—not apparently from any wish to ridicule
him, but unable to resist the temptation and infection".[2]
Mr Shelly writes, "A Roman crowd, Cicero tells us,
would applaud a well-turned sentence for its pleasant
sound, just as an English audience will applaud a
striking argument or a happy illustration".[3]

From general remarks such as these, and for ordinary
purposes, it is sufficient to define rhythm as the organisation of perceptions in an orderly way, and rhythmical
material as that which is capable of being so organised.
But many difficulties attend the study of rhythm in its
particular manifestations. The precise nature of the
rhythm of speech, with which we are concerned here,

[1] W. M. Patterson, *The Rhythm of Prose*, p. xxi (Columbia Univ.
Press, New York, 1917).

[2] G. Saintsbury, *History of English Prose Rhythm*, p. 7 (London,
1912).

[3] J. Shelly, "Rhythmical Prose in Latin and English", in *Church
Quarterly Review*, April 1912, p. 88.

has proved to be a most controversial subject, and, before
drawing any conclusions, an attempt will be made to
give some of the views held by different scholars.

THEORIES AND THEORISTS OF
SPEECH-RHYTHM

At least three, and probably four, main theories can
be distinguished.

I. The "Quantivists" believe that speech-rhythm is
based on the relationship of syllabic quantities, that is,
that the time durations of certain syllables are long,
and of others short, by nature or position, and that,
although stress may be superimposed, English verse is
primarily based on a regular recurrence and pattern
formation of these quantities. Classical Greek and Latin
verse was based on quantity; there was recurrence of
long and short syllables according to a definite pattern.
Moreover, it is generally allowed that the durations of
these syllables bore a definite numerical relationship to
one another, but the "Quantivists" do not assert that
this obtains in English verse. For them, syllabic duration is the factor which determines rhythm, and every
syllable may be classed as "long" or "short" without
implying that the "short" is normally a certain fraction
of the "long".

Two difficulties of this theory should be noticed here.
In English speech, the length of a syllable often varies
according to the context in which it is placed. The

other difficulty concerns the perception of durations, and will be discussed below.[1]

II. A second group of theorists, among whom the name of Sidney Lanier[2] is important, believe that the manifestation of rhythm in music and verse is the same and obeys common laws. They agree with the "Quantivists" that duration is the primary element of rhythm, but direct their attention to duration of feet rather than of syllables. Like bars in music, feet in verse are to be equal in duration, and syllable grouping is to be effected accordingly. With the notable exception of Lanier, many of these theorists insist that the foot in verse, like the bar in music, should begin with a strong stress, thus assuming that iambic and anapaestic rhythms are the same as trochaic and dactylic respectively.

III. In its assertion that accent is the sole principle that regulates English verse, the "Sectionalist" theory differs fundamentally from those described above. It is usually associated with Edwin Guest,[3] who abandons scansion by feet and substitutes a division by sections similar to that obtaining in Old English alliterative verse. The sections are determined by the stresses. This theory attaches the greatest importance to the number of strong stresses in verse-lines.

IV. The theory of rhythm relied upon in the following

[1] pp. 11–12.
[2] *The Science of English Verse* (New York, 1880 and 1886).
[3] *History of English Rhythms* (London, 1838).

pages corresponds with that of a group of theorists who differ from all these.

Let us begin by considering any series of auditory events such as, for example, the ticking of a clock. This may be, and, with many clocks, is, rhythmical. Now let us suppose that the ticks are identical with each other in every way, and that they occur at perfectly regular intervals of time, thus:

.   .   -   .   .   .   .   etc.

It is very doubtful whether this series can be recognised as being rhythmical. It can be organised as rhythmical by the mind, but the result will be entirely subjective; it will not be influenced in any way by the series.[1] The rhythm thus produced exists only in the hearer's mind, and may vary with each individual because there is nothing in the material to suggest any particular rhythm. As Mr Egerton Smith writes, "When...a regularly periodic series of unvarying sounds presents itself which is not perceptibly marked off into groups or sections, there is always a tendency for subjective rhythm to arise. The instinct of rhythm is so firmly rooted in human nature that it will lead to the involuntary formation of rhythmical groups even where originally there were none; i.e. where the stimuli did not vary objectively".[2]

[1] Mr Sonnenschein asserts that he can divide isosyllabic verse into rhythm groups, but such grouping would be either subjective or merely by eye.

[2] *Principles of English Metre*, pp. 9–10.

If, however, the ticks are not identical, some becoming louder, or longer, or in any way different from the others, they tend to form themselves into groups and, as soon as repetition takes place, a particular rhythm begins to be suggested to the mind, and the material may be recognised as being rhythmical. Thus, for example, the following may result:

.   .   .   .   etc.

A single group (e.g. . .) would not be sufficient to determine the character of the rhythm, but repetition need not be regular, and there need be no fixed limit to the intervals between recurrent groups.

Auditory rhythm may therefore be defined simply as *the organisation of sound stimulated in the mind by the repetition of a series or group of auditory events in time.*

Psychologists point out that, strictly speaking, rhythm exists in the mind and is a particular organisation or response stimulated by rhythmical material. It is, however, convenient to refer to that arrangement of sounds in the material which stimulates the particular effect as the "rhythm" of the material and, if the strict application of the term be not overlooked, little harm will be done.

"Rhythm", writes Mr Egerton Smith, "involves continuity—'a flowing': the occurrence of two similar feet may set up a rhythm, which will be confirmed by a third, but, as Poe observed, 'in a line of one foot we can have no appreciation of Rhythm'".[1]

[1] *Principles of English Metre*, p. 63.

Space of time is not comprehensible to the mind unless there is some mark by which it may be recognised, this mark, in the case of auditory rhythm, being a time-occupying sound. Thus it is impossible to say that, because the series of identical sounds

.   .   .   .   etc.

is a repetition of groups which are each composed of a sound and a space of time, therefore it is rhythmical. Such a group would not be recognisable to the human ear. No group can consist of a sound followed by a space of time, for the space of time is infinite unless broken by another sound. Space in time does not become recognisable to the ear until it is marked by a sound. The sounds, therefore, are the factors which make rhythm possible, and it is their relationship which must be considered.

Sound itself occupies time. The amount of time occupied by a sound is called its time duration, or simply its duration. In classical Greek and Latin the durations, or "quantities", of syllables were rigid; certain syllables were long, others short, either by nature or position. In music, except in "tempo rubato", the time durations of different notes bear a fixed relationship to each other throughout the piece (e.g. a minim = two crotchets, etc.). In English speech, however, this is not so. The length of (that is, the time taken to pronounce) any given syllable varies according to the context, and may vary continually throughout a whole piece of speech.

Mr Omond tells us that quantity in Greek and Latin

verse "referred solely to the time syllables took to pronounce...this was held to depend either on vowel-
duration, or on retardation by separately pronounced
consonants....In English we have nothing analogous to
this fixed rule....We have a powerful stress-accent,
which reduces quantitative distinction to low and fluc-
tuating values; they, apparently, had a very slight
one".[1]

Professor Abercrombie writes:

The natural English rhythms are accentual—if quantity enters
at all into the rhythms natural to English, it only does so subordinate to, and in a manner prescribed by, accent. This, of
course, is not to identify quantity with accent; but a quantitative
pattern running counter to an accentual rhythm would in English
not be heard without special and studious cultivation of a sense
for quantity....Thus English rhythms may properly be regarded
as accentual in scheme; quantity being employed not schemati-
cally, but occasionally, following the requirements of accent....
But quantity is commonly used in English versification not
rhythmically at all but as a syllabic quality, like alliteration
and assonance; and its effect is frequently inextricable from the
effect of, for example, sequences of vowels or consonants. Thus
in the line
                "In *Ce*dar, *Ma*rble, *I*vory, or *Go*ld"
the rhythm is given by the four accents in the italicised vowel
sounds, and the rhythmic character requires no assistance from
the quantity of these vowels; the first of them, for example,
being of the same quantity as the unaccented syllables which
precede and follow it. But apart from the rhythm which the

[1] T. S. Omond, *English Metrists, 18th and 19th Centuries*, p. 2
(Oxford, 1907).

accented vowels establish, the mere syllabic quality of their sequence is conspicuous, and the quantity—"length"—of each vowel is heard only as a feature of their syllabic quality—of their nature as "front" or "back", "tense" or "slack", "rounded" or "unrounded" vowels, but not as a feature of their place in a rhythmic scheme; and average hearing probably no more notices their quantity in the general phonetic effect than it notices such qualities as analysis labels "front", "tense", and the rest. Prosody is not concerned with syllabic quantities except as they specifically enter into rhythmic schematism: and with this very occasional exception, quantity does not therefore belong to the prosody of natural English rhythms.[1]

Every articulate sound exhibits three characteristics:

(a) Stress or "force of breath impulse initiating syllables".[2]

(b) Quantity or duration of time (i.e. the time occupied by the syllable).

(c) Pitch or tone (i.e. position in the musical scale).

No single one of these can exist alone. Thus it cannot be said that *either* stress, *or* quantity, *or* pitch alone gives rhythm. They are all present but, though quantity and pitch are present, the normal basis of English speech-rhythm is one of stress. In any prose sentence such as the following,

I cannot be sorry to have forced Mr Kingsley to bring out in fulness his charges against me;[3]

[1] Lascelles Abercrombie, *The Principles of English Prosody*, Part I, pp. 22–4 (London, 1923).

[2] *Ibid.* p. 19.

[3] J. H. Newman, *Apologia pro Vita Sua*—opening sentence.

or in lines of verse,

> St Agnes' Eve—Ah, bitter chill it was!
> The owl, for all his feathers, was a-cold,[1]

almost every reader is conscious of the stress laid on the different syllables long before he is conscious of their durations, and still longer before he recognises their relative durations. The pitch may vary according to the voice of the reader whilst the rhythm remains the same. Thus, the rhythm of the sentence, phrase, or whatever it may be, is determined by the stress. It must be so, since the perception of stress in almost every reader of English speech predominates over, and comes before, the perception of syllable duration. It is frequently found that increase of stress is accompanied by increase in duration, but this does not necessarily occur, as we have just seen in Professor Abercrombie's example,

> In Cedar, Marble, Ivory, or Gold,

where the difference in duration, if any, between the stressed vowel in each word and the syllables which immediately precede or follow it is very slight. As Mr Egerton Smith writes, " weight may be composed of speech-accent with either quantity or pitch or both; and...its constituents may vary in their mutual proportions at different times, e.g. stress may be combined with length and low pitch or with shortness and high pitch".[2] English speech-rhythm, therefore, is

---

[1] Keats, *Eve of St Agnes.*

[2] *Principles of English Metre*, p. 13.

primarily based upon stress, and, though quantity, in the sense of duration, does enter, since all sounds occupy time, it is subordinate to stress.

In many books the word "accent" is used as an alternative for "stress". Strictly speaking, these are not synonymous. "Accent" really denotes the combination of both pitch and stress. But, since increase in stress usually produces a higher pitch, the two generally go together. Thus, when English speech-rhythm is spoken of as being primarily "accentual", the meaning is that it is determined by stress.

So far then, there have been established two fundamental theses on which the study of the rhythm of prose is based:

(a) That auditory rhythm is the organisation of sound stimulated in the mind by the repetition of a series or group of auditory events in time.

(b) That English speech-rhythm is primarily determined by stress.

THE RHYTHM OF PROSE

It is now necessary to consider the particular application of the definition of rhythm to prose. The definition states that repetition of some kind is essential to rhythm but the intervals at which repetition may take place are not defined and may be irregular. There is obviously no difficulty in applying this to poetry, but, at first sight, "prose-rhythm" may seem to be a

contradiction of terms and it must be proved that this
is not so.

The materials of English speech-rhythm are syllables
bearing different degrees of stress which fall into three
broad divisions: strong, weak, and secondary, stress.[1]
In the poorest, most pedestrian, and inharmonious prose
these materials are only recognisable with considerable
difficulty and even then they are not definite. In this
kind of prose, blocks of many syllables frequently occur
in which the stresses are indefinite and scansion not only
difficult but impossible to carry out with any degree of
certainty. Rhythmical or "numerous" prose, however,
tends very largely to scan itself; there is little difficulty
in marking with certainty the distribution of stress. In
a like manner poetry also admits of definite scansion.
Furthermore, there is in "numerous" prose, as in poetry,
a distinct grouping of syllables into blocks which we
call "feet".[2]

From this point confusion begins. Professor Saintsbury maintains that "variety" is the principle of prose-
rhythm. The word "variety" usually implies variation
from something, but Professor Saintsbury does not
appear to mean this. His "variety" is rather an abstract
"continual difference", the complete absence of any
tendency towards regularity. If this assertion that
variety is the principle of prose-rhythm is true, then
surely prose-rhythm is not rhythm at all, for it is very
doubtful whether completely irregular material can

[1] See below, pp. 17–18.   [2] See below, p. 18.

suggest rhythm. There is, however, another principle of prose-rhythm which is equal in importance to that of variety, and this is the principle of recurrence, which, as we have seen, is necessary to the suggestion of rhythm. Recurrence is present, but not as in metre, and the difference must be carefully considered.

Recurrence in metre occurs at such short intervals that it becomes so insistent as to form a pattern which persists throughout all modulations. The pattern is so definite to the ear, that the reader *expects* it, and, more or less consciously, refers all modulations to it as a base or norm. This expectancy is essentially a metrical element. In "numerous" prose there is recurrence at intervals, which are longer than in poetry, and irregular, thus there is no expectancy; when recurrence is so insistent as to beget expectancy, then prose ceases to be prose and becomes metrical or quasi-metrical. Examples of this will be found below. In prose there is recurrence but no base or "norm". There is also variety, in Professor Saintsbury's sense of the term, not as a variation from a base.

Recurrence in prose appears in many forms. It will be shown that prose often has a suggestion of almost metrical regularity, especially in those groups of syllables called "cadences"[1] which, though to a certain extent metrical in principle, "are not", as Professor Elton says, "metrical combinations".[2] These groups are

[1] See below, chap. III.

[2] O. Elton, "English Prose Numbers", in *Essays and Studies of the English Association*, IV, p. 52 (Oxford, 1913).

recognisable as soon as they appear, but in good prose they do not recur on a fixed system (as, for example, do rhymes in poetry) because this would induce expectancy and tend to become metrical. Nevertheless, they provide elements of law and order. Also, in carefully balanced prose there is a certain correspondence of the members of sentences in length or in number of strong stresses.[1] Finally, the prose-feet themselves are often " graded " in various ways.[2] These are the chief elements of recurrence in prose, and Professor Elton sums them up as follows:

If, then, we ask what are the elements of rhythm, that is, of law, order and recurrence, which are to be found in English prose amidst its infinite variety, they may be classified for the present into the following : First, those successions of feet defined by the "foot-scansion" and consisting of entire words, that may be grouped under such a principle as "gradation". Secondly, the bursts shorter rather than longer, of actual metre, that is of verse-feet, which are not necessarily made up of entire words. Thirdly, the cadences, coming at the end of groups, clauses or sentences, and of recurrent but not of metrical type; yet having in common with metre the fact that they also may strike across the word-divisions. These cadences are either classical in origin (*cursus*) or native ; the former having been classified, the latter still awaiting full classification.[3]

Some theorists, such as Mr Patterson,[4] endeavour to

[1] See below, chap. II, p. 68.

[2] See below, chap. II, p. 55, *et passim*.

[3] O. Elton, "English Prose Numbers", in *A Sheaf of Papers*, pp. 187–8 (Liverpool Univ. Press, 1922).

[4] W. M. Patterson, *The Rhythm of Prose* (Columbia Univ. Press, New York, 1917).

explain the rhythm of prose as being a kind of elaborate syncopation. This, however, is unsatisfactory, as there must be first of all a definite scheme on which to base the syncopation. There is no such scheme in prose. Modulation in verse may be in some ways analogous to syncopation in music, but variety in prose, never.

Thus, there can be, and is, rhythm in prose; a rhythm which is sometimes smooth, limpid, and flowing, sometimes rushing and tumultuous, and which satisfies the ear by its harmony and completeness. In its best form it is continuous rather than antiphonic; a too close correspondence of its parts tends towards monotony. For this reason alone, if not for any other, such hybrid forms as the stave poetry of Ossian are not true prose. Finally, though there are elements of recurrence, of law and order, in "numerous" prose, there is, or should be, nothing to suggest expectancy. As soon as particular rhythms are expected in particular places we leave the realms of prose and enter those of metre.

SCANSION

Before going further, it will be convenient here to formulate a satisfactory system of symbols which will be used in scansion. Having rejected the "quantivist" and musical theories of English speech-rhythm, it follows that neither the old classical signs, " – " and " ⌣ " for long and short syllables respectively, nor the notation of music, can be used with consistency. Moreover, it is not proposed to add to the difficulties of anyone who is approaching the subject of prose-rhythm for the first time, by making use of an elaborate system of scansion such as that adopted by Mr Egerton Smith in *The Principles of English Metre*. It seems advisable to limit as much as possible the number of symbols used and, for denoting degrees of stress, three alone will suffice in practice:

(1) "⁄", denoting strong stress, e.g.

Chánge into extrémity is very fréquent and eásy.[1]

(2) "ᵛ", denoting secondary stress. This occupies an intermediate position between strong and weak stress. It is distinctly heavier than the latter, but lighter than the former. For example, in the following phrase,

But the quíncunx of héaven rŭns lów,[2]

"runs" is distinctly stressed; it is not a light syllable like "but", "the", "of", but it is not so heavy as "quin-", "heav-", and "low". Thus its stress is termed "secondary". In English prose, whenever more than three light syllables follow one another, secondary stress begins to be set up as in this example given by Professor Elton:[3] "and ĭf it were so". Mr Fijn van Draat writes: "Skeat goes so far as to say: 'Never use three consecutive weak syllables, unless you desire to ruin your verse'. And he might have added 'and your prose'. For no rhythmical prose is possible when many unstrest words come together; if

---

[1] Ben Jonson, *Discoveries*, II *Casus*.

[2] Sir T. Browne, *Garden of Cyrus*, chap. v.

[3] "English Prose Numbers", in *A Sheaf of Papers*, p. 134.

they do, some stress is involuntarily laid on one of them, unless the sense prohibits it ".[1] However, this would deny the existence of most paeons (see below, p. 42), whereas the paeon is one of the staple feet of English numerous prose. It is when more than three consecutive light syllables occur that secondary stress tends to be set up.

(3) "×", denoting weak stress. This sign is used only when feet are quoted without the text; whenever the text is quoted, weak syllables are left unmarked.

In any logical sequence of speech-sounds the syllables tend to arrange themselves in different groups, and a more definite separation is noticed between the groups than between the individual sounds composing a group. Thus in the following sentence,

The eldest | of the three | is named | Mater : Lachrymarum, | —Our Lady | of Tears,[2]

the separations are the most pronounced at the places marked by vertical lines. In analysis we call these groups "feet", and mark them off by vertical lines. As a rule, in every foot, there is at least one strongly stressed syllable round which the other syllables tend to group themselves.[3]

Now, one of the main differences between poetry and

[1] P. Fijn van Draat, *Rhythm in English Prose*, p. 13.

[2] De Quincey, *Suspiria de Profundis* (*Works*, ed. D. Masson, XIII, p. 365, London, 1897).

[3] Feet of the type × × are rare in poetry, and not admitted by some scholars. They are still more rare, if ever present, in prose.

prose is that, in the former there is continuous repetition and variation of a rhythmical pattern or scheme, whereas in prose this is not so. According to Professor Abercrombie, "the nature of metre requires a line either to consist of one rhythmic element several times repeated, or to be itself a repeating order of varying rhythmic elements. When the rhythm is given by accents, these elements will either be accents, or accents with non-accents attached; and since we are merely considering sentences of rhythm without regard to their syntax, there is no reason why these elements should be whole or single words".[1] The pattern is insistent and can be heard throughout its modulations. Thus, in verse, the foot-divisions frequently cut the words, as, for example, in

For mán|y a pét|ty kíng | ere Ár|thur cáme.[2]

But, in prose there is no such definite and insistent pattern and therefore it will be readily understood that the grouping of syllables is entirely logical; it is regulated by the development of the thought or the exposition of the argument. Herein lies an important (perhaps *the* important) difference between prose and verse. The absence, in prose, of a regular repeating rhythmical pattern allows division according to syntax (i.e. logical grouping) to predominate, whereas, in verse, the insistence of the metrical pattern causes metrical grouping to predominate over logical. In highly numer-

[1] Lascelles Abercrombie, *Principles of English Prosody*, Part I, p. 67 (London, 1923).
[2] Tennyson, *The Coming of Arthur*, l. 5.

ous prose, cadence (in which foot-divisions may cut the
words[1]) is constantly coming to the front; in blank verse
which is closely packed with thought, as, for example,
some of Shakespeare's later work, and in free verse,
logical groups are constantly coming forward. Thus, in
scanning prose, where logical groups predominate, the
foot-divisions never cut across the words. The following
is an example:

You háve, | indéed, | wínged | mínisters | of véngeance, | who
cárry | your bólts | in their póunces | to the remótest | vérge |
of the séa.[2]

We now come to the naming of the feet themselves.
In prose four main types of rhythm can be distinguished:

(a) Rhythm of the type ×ı, ××ı or ×ıı, ××ıı, etc.,
beginning with one or more weakly stressed syllables
and rising to one or more strongly stressed syllables.
This may be termed *rising* rhythm.

(b) Rhythm of the type ıx, ıxx, or ııx, ııxx, etc.,
where each foot begins with one or more strongly
stressed syllables and falls to one or more weakly
stressed syllables. This may be termed *falling* rhythm.

(c) Rhythm of the type ×ıx, ××ıx, or ıxı, ıxxı, or
×ııx, etc., where each foot begins and ends on the same
kind of stress, and contains both strong and weak
stresses. This type may be termed *waved* rhythm.

[1] See below, chap. iii, p. 88.
[2] Burke, *On Conciliation with America*, p. 24 (ed. H. Lamont,
Boston, 1897).

(d) Rhythm of the type ′, or ″, or ‴, where each foot is wholly made up of strong stresses. This may be termed *level* rhythm.

With the help of the terms *rising* and *falling* rhythm it would be a simple matter to name such feet as ×′ or ××′ or ′×× by calling them two- or three-syllable feet containing one strong stress, in *rising* or *falling* rhythm as the case may be. But this is very clumsy, involving as it does the use of cumbersome phrases, and it would be much more convenient if single words could be substituted for them. Moreover, the difficulty increases enormously when it is necessary to describe feet in *waved* rhythm, as, for example, ×′×× or ×‴×, etc. It is, therefore, much more convenient to have a series of words by which the different feet can be described. The ancient writers of Greece and Rome had these names, and there is no reason why we should not adopt them for our feet also, if, in so doing, an essential difference is not forgotten.

It must be remembered that, in classical rhythms, the syllables bore a definite time-relationship to one another; some were long and others short in duration. It has been shown that the natural English rhythms are not quantitative, and therefore the classical names can only be used by us with this proviso; that their use does not pre-suppose acceptance of the "quantivist" theory, or, indeed, any other classical theory of metre, the terms being used solely for the sake of convenience as they have no manageable alternatives in English.

In order that the student may, with minimum difficulty, familiarise himself with the names of the different feet, they are given below in the form of a table:

Feet of two syllables	Feet of three syllables	Feet of four syllables		Feet of five syllables
iamb ×′ trochee ′× spondee ″	anapaest ××′ dactyl ′×× molossus ‴ amphibrach ×′× cretic ′×′ bacchius ″× anti-bacchius ×″	paeons (4 forms) 4 syllables with one strong stress	1st ′××× 2nd ×′×× 3rd ××′× 4th ×××′	"dochmiacs" (numerous varieties)
		antispast ×″× choriamb ′××′ "ionic a minore" ××″ "ionic a majore" ″×× di-iamb ×′×′ di-trochee ′×′× epitrites (4 forms) 4 syllables with three strong stresses	×‴ ′×″ ″×′ ‴×	

Note. As Professor Saintsbury says, the dochmiac is "A foot of five syllables, in which the possible permutations of long and short[1] give a very large number of varieties. In English prose those containing two long and three short are perhaps the commonest, arranged in their different combinations. One long and four short, similarly varied, is not uncommon; and three longs with two shorts intervening may be found; but more than three longs, I think, never".[2] Professor Elton

[1] That is to say "strong" and "weak" syllables. Professor Saintsbury's terms and symbols frequently differ from those used here.

[2] *History of English Prose Rhythm*, Table of feet facing p. 1.

regards them "as one or other kind of paeon with a light syllable for preface".[1]

Monosyllables are common in English, the syllable necessarily bearing a strong stress.

To the above list Professor Saintsbury would add "pyrrhic" (××), "tribrach" (×××), "proceleusmatic" (××××), "di-spondee" (////), but the presence of these in English prose appears to be very doubtful.

Professor Elton comments on the tendency of epitrites to break up into feet, and this is also noticeable in such groups as the di-iamb, di-trochee, and molossus. This tendency to split up occurs in nearly all groups containing more than two strongly stressed syllables.[2]

Only very occasionally do we find feet of more than five syllables; beyond this limit there is a marked tendency to split up into smaller groups, though the point of separation may not always be well defined. The following is a good example:

Whèn : they were creáted | abòve : the horízon | with the sún, | òr : there was nŏt : an éye | to behóld them.[3]

However, as Professor Saintsbury writes, "It is possible that, especially in certain kinds of prose of low tension, blocks of even six syllables may, by the help of something like slur, assume the position of feet".[4]

---

[1] "English Prose Numbers", in *A Sheaf of Papers*, p. 133.

[2] See below, chap. II, p. 39.

[3] Sir T. Browne, *Garden of Cyrus*, chap. IV (ed. Bohn, II, p. 551, London, 1878).

[4] *History of English Prose Rhythm*, p. 478.

At this point a word of caution should be given. Scansion can never be rigid. Different people might scan the same passage with varying results, yet each scansion would be, for the person who made it, an accurate representation of the rhythm of that passage. In practice, however, the differences are surprisingly slight. The accented syllables are usually so well marked, in numerous prose, that they are the same for every hearer. It must be made clear that the scansion in this book represents the writer's perception of the rhythm of the different passages; the reader may, and in some cases probably will, scan differently. Nevertheless, it is unlikely that the importance of the results obtained will be impaired.

PROSE-RHYTHM: THEORIES AND THEORISTS

A. *Classical*

Rhythm has long been recognised as an important feature of prose. In the *Rhetoric*, Aristotle speaks of prose as "neither possessing metre, nor destitute of rhythm",[1] and proceeds to indicate the paeon as the base of prose-rhythm. Dionysius, in the *De Compositione*, states that "no rhythm whatever is banished from un-metred composition, any more than from that in metre". Quintilian (*Inst. Orat.*) goes still further, telling us that the appearance of verse in prose is "the ugliest fault of

[1] *Vide* Saintsbury, *History of English Prose Rhythm*, to which I am indebted for this account of classical theorists.

all", but, he adds, "actual verses often escape us without our perceiving them". The importance of this remark will readily be recognised. Modern investigation has endeavoured to discover why these "verses escape us", and the most reasonable explanation seems to be that the metrical tendency is subdued by the well-defined prose-feet, a statement which will be more fully explained below.[1] Quintilian also insists on the principle of variety in prose-rhythm; "no system will be good if...it go always on the *same* feet", and, with a certain effect of quaintness, he says "the management of feet in prose is *more* difficult than in verse".

Concerning prose-rhythm in particular, Cicero says little that is new. His best remarks concern the dochmiac, and he states interestingly "that by pause you can destroy the bad effect of a continuous iambic run". He is essentially the orator, and, as such, pays most attention to sentence endings. Herein lies his chief importance for our present purpose, but discussion of cadence is reserved for a future chapter (chap. III).

With a mention of Longinus this brief notice of classical criticism of prose-rhythm must close. Longinus condemns the trochee as degrading, but this has no application to English prose because the very nature of the language renders many of its rhythms trochaic.

Further details of classical theorists of prose-rhythm are unnecessary here, and we may now consider the results of some modern investigation in the subject.

[1] See chap. II, *passim.*

B. *Modern*

There does not appear to be, in English, any book which may do for the study of English prose-rhythm[1] what Mr Omond's *English Metrists* (Oxford, 1920) has already done for verse. Compared with prosody, the scientific study of prose-rhythm in English is of comparatively recent growth, but even now there would seem to be room for such a chronicle of theorists as Mr Omond's, and, until one appears, the student must be satisfied with such stray facts as he can glean in the course of his reading. For the present, it is proposed merely to indicate some of the most important modern theorists and theories of prose-rhythm without regard to chronological order.

One of the most illuminating of modern writings on the subject is Professor Elton's *English Prose Numbers*, first published in *Essays and Studies of the English Association* (vol. IV, 1913) and re-published with other essays by Professor Elton in *A Sheaf of Papers* (Liverpool U.P. 1922), to which frequent reference has been, and will be, made throughout this book. The paper is short, but the exposition it gives is clear and full of suggestion. Avoiding the vexed question of the nature of rhythm,

---

[1] There are other accounts of modern investigation of prose-rhythm. A recent interesting account of Latin prose-rhythm written in French, by M. François Novotný (*État Actuel des Études sur le Rhythme de la Prose Latine*, Lwów, 1929), was lent to the present writer, who wishes to take this opportunity of expressing his gratitude and thanks to the lender.

Professor Elton gives us the key to his conception of
prose-rhythm almost immediately: "An English prose
sentence, for the present purpose, consists of a number
of *feet*, or groups of words, containing at least one
accent in each foot, but sometimes two accents. In verse,
the feet may and constantly do cut across the words
('My bós|om's lórd'). In prose, the foot, as here de-
fined, must begin with the beginning and end with
the end of a word, though not necessarily of the same
word; the prose-feet would be 'My bósom's | lord'...".[1]
There are also important remarks on cadence and on
the relationship between prose and verse which will be
mentioned below.

Dr MacColl, in "Rhythm in English Verse, Prose and
Speech", published in *Essays and Studies of the English
Association* (vol. v, 1914), criticises Professor Elton's
logical grouping of syllables, stating that prose-rhythm
so defined "is not a rhythm at all, but something else.... .
It is the *logical* distribution of the syllables into their
smaller groups, in which words are never broken up.
And not being a rhythmical division (except in so far as
each logical group has a chief logical accent coinciding
with a rhythmical accent), this system cannot serve as
an account of the rhythm of prose, though the distinction does hold the clue to the definition of prose".[2]

Dr MacColl, it should be noticed, has to admit that
"each logical group has a chief logical accent coinciding
with a rhythmical accent"; then why should not these

[1] Section i, §1. [2] p. 35.

logical groups be also rhythm-groups? According to the definition given above (p. 7) any series of varying sounds which contains some degree of recurrence can be organised as rhythmical, and, in speech, these sounds are syllables bearing different degrees of stress, no matter how or why the stress is given. Professor Elton's groups then are rhythm-groups, they are not mere divisions by eye but are immediately recognisable by ear. They are present in verse, but in verse the metrical pattern is so insistent that they are usually subdued. In this line,

      The cúr|few tólls | the knéll | of pár|ting dáy,

the prose-feet would be,

      The cúrfew | tólls | the knéll | of párting | dáy,

but the metrical pattern is so regular as to predominate over and subdue the prose-feet. In prose, the prose-feet exist side by side with the cadences,[1] which, though not metrical in form, in common with metre may, and frequently do, cut the words, and increase or diminish in accordance with the more or less "numerous" character of the prose. The two systems can be perceived separately by the mind, even though they may not be heard separately as registered on a sound-recording instrument. Dr MacColl goes too far in rejecting these prose-feet.

Dr MacColl may, indeed, be numbered among the musical theorists and, consequently, his views on prose-

            [1] See below, chap. III, p. 88.

rhythm differ considerably from those of Professors Elton
and Saintsbury. In his paper he devotes most of his space
to criticising these two writers, and gives little con-
structive theorising on his own account. What he does
give, however, is important. He states that prose, like
verse, has the recurrence of equal feet, that is to say of
feet equal in duration, but not the recurrence of the
same feet, or of equal numbers of feet, or of a pattern
of feet. He views the relationship between prose and
verse as a kind of chain, at the extreme ends of which
are "characteristic prose" and "characteristic verse",
linked together by "numerous prose" and "verse invaded by prose emphasis". He defines the four as
follows :[1]

Characteristic prose : free resolution of bar, with no predomi-
nance of foot, or recurrence of feet at the end of lines. Variation
in length of line.

Numerous prose : less free and frequent resolution, so that
rhythm becomes more apparent. Tendency to recurrence of lines
with the same number of bars.

Verse invaded by prose emphasis : frequent resolution of feet
in early bars, and occasional in later. Length of line may be
irregular.

Characteristic verse : resolution rare and rarest towards the
end of lines. Lines of same length or of recurrent pattern.

"In typical prose, as distinguished from poetical or
oratorical set pieces, like Browne's or De Quincey's,
rhythmical structure, though existing, is not brought

[1] p. 50.

to the front, but takes a secondary place in consciousness.[1] This is as far as Dr MacColl goes; he does not take the next step which would lead him to cadence, as distinct from prose-rhythm, specially studied by Professors Clark and Elton, Mr Croll and Mr Shelly.[2]

In his *History of English Prose Rhythm* (London, 1912), Professor Saintsbury occasionally allows prose-foot divisions to cut the words, but, apart from these rare exceptions, his feet always begin with the beginning and end with the end of a word. Sometimes words occur which, on account of their tendency to split up, present extraordinary difficulty. These are usually long, containing several syllables, of which two or even three frequently bear strong stress, and are to be found commonly in writers such as Browne who show a marked preference for a Latinised vocabulary. The word "oneirocritical", so much used by Browne, provides a good example. Professor Saintsbury writes: "There is no objection to the falling of a foot-end in the middle of a word. But it is less frequent in prose than in verse; and its comparative rarity perhaps furnishes one of the differences between prose- and verse-rhythm".[3]

Professor Saintsbury, however, devotes little space to theorising. He is not concerned, in this book, with the nature of rhythm in general, or of prose-rhythm in particular. His chief business is the scansion of representative passages from the work of different authors

[1] p. 46.   [2] See below, chap. III, p. 73.
[3] p. 479.

together with comments on their rhythmical usages so as to provide a chronological survey of the rhythm of English prose. In this way he furnishes an immense amount of valuable data for the student and has provided a storehouse to which the present writer, in common with many others, is greatly indebted. Professor Saintsbury adheres to the quantitative symbols in scansion but his terms "long" and "short" do not appear to have any meaning connected with duration but are actually equivalent to "heavy" and "light" or "strong" and "weak" stress respectively. During his analysis of selected passages, many general observations on the rhythm of prose are called forth, and are tabulated in an appendix (pp. 478–82). One of these has just been quoted; another, which will be quoted now and to which reference has already been made,[1] seems to furnish the key to Professor Saintsbury's conception of prose-rhythm:

The great principle of foot arrangement in prose, and of Prose Rhythm, is variety.[2]

Mr Fijn van Draat (*Rhythm in English Prose*, Heidelberg, 1910) does not attempt to define, or to advance theories of, prose-rhythm. His book is mainly concerned with a detailed exposition of how the order of words is affected by rhythm, and turns on the author's thesis that "The first and essential condition for the securing of rhythmical movement is the avoidance of

[1] See above, p. 13.   [2] p. 478.

two strest syllables in immediate succession",[1] a statement which, in view of the effective use by many
writers of the clashing of strong stress,[2] seems to be too
sweeping and uncompromising.

There are, however, one or two remarks which demand
notice here. The following statement is important:

> It should be borne in mind that Rhythm always means *re-
> petition*. It is—to give a single instance—impossible to deter-
> mine the rhythm of the words: *to forgive* taken by themselves.
> Is it ⊥×⊥; or rather ×× ⊥? All depends upon what follows or
> what precedes.[3]

Mr Fijn van Draat considers that "Rhythm-groups
mostly consist of words logically belonging together
welded into a closer union by means of the metrical
flow".[4] He goes on to say that rhythmical prose does
not mean unbroken rhythmical movement, but prose
that shows a tendency to form rhythm-groups.

Mr W. M. Patterson's book *The Rhythm of Prose*
(New York, 1917) is a detailed investigation of the
nature of prose-rhythm from a psychological point of
view, supplemented by many interesting laboratory
experiments, but it does not bring us much nearer to a
clear understanding or appreciation of prose-rhythm.
His theory seems to be that the rhythm of prose corresponds to a very elaborate scheme of syncopation in
music, a scheme which, if carried out in music, would

---

[1] p. 9.   [2] See below, pp. 55–6.
[3] p. 7.   [4] p. 14.

render the normal time base unrecognisable to the human ear. Moreover, though laboratory experiments are undoubtedly valuable, it should be remembered that no sound-recording instrument can show the exact response of the human brain to a series of sounds.

Stray remarks on prose-rhythm are to be found scattered up and down most treatises on prosody or on the nature of rhythm in general. With a brief notice of one of these this chapter must close. Mr Egerton Smith, to whose book, *The Principles of English Metre*, frequent references have already been made, endeavours to point out one or two of the differences between prose and verse. However, his assertion that rhythmical movement necessitates the occurrence of stress at fairly regular intervals does not allow him to do justice to prose. Thus, he writes, " Doubtless in many prose passages the syllables which are stressed as having great mental importance are separated in reading by fairly regular intervals of time. And indeed some inquirers think they can find a rhythmical tendency in all language; but in prose it is, in a passage of any considerable length, usually no more than a tendency and is quite unobtrusive, only to be found when we look for it, and even then often only by some straining. In poetry, on the other hand, rhythmical movement seems inevitable and cannot be overlooked ".[1] Rhythmical movement cannot, however, be overlooked in " numerous " prose but is one of its most prominent characteristics; it is

[1] pp. 18–19.

certainly more than a " tendency " to be found " only
by some straining " in such works as the *Authorised
Version of the Bible*, or in those of Jeremy Taylor, or
De Quincey, or Sir Thomas Browne.

The above, then, are some of the chief theorists and
theories of prose-rhythm. All question of cadence and
cursus has been reserved for a future chapter (chap. III).
By the discussion and statement of these theories and
by the formulation of a theory of rhythm and a system
of scansion the writer hopes to have established a foun-
dation upon which the remainder of this book can be
built. It is now possible to examine in some detail the
rhythm of English prose.

CHAPTER II

PROSE-RHYTHM

THE rhythm of prose is made up of two elements, closely woven in the best prose, yet always distinguishable; prose-rhythm, which is the subject of this chapter, and cadence, which is reserved for the next. In the preceding chapter it was shown[1] that since, in prose, there is no metrical pattern to cause interference with the normal speech accents, the basic syllable-grouping is logical, whereas it is metrical in verse. From this it follows that, as a general rule, the rhythm-groups of prose are composed of whole words, and, therefore, in scansion the words are never cut by the foot-divisions. "An English prose sentence", writes Professor Elton, "for the present purpose,[2] consists of a number of *feet*, or groups of words, containing at least one accent in each foot, but sometimes two accents.[3] In verse, the feet may and constantly do cut across the words ('My bós|om's lórd'). In prose, the foot, as here defined, must begin with the beginning and end with the end of a word, though not necessarily of the same word; the

[1] pp. 18-20.

[2] I.e. for the purpose of analysis of prose-rhythm.

[3] And, it may be added, sometimes three accents (*e.g.* epitrites). But three consecutive strong stresses tend to separate rather than to combine to form a foot, hence the rarity of both the epitrite and the molossus in English prose.

prose-feet would be 'My bósom's | lord'...".[1] This is prose-rhythm as distinct from cadence. Discussion of cadence, if entered upon here, would confuse the issue; it will be sufficient for the student to remember that cadence is a name for special rhythmical sequences[2] which are quite distinct from prose-feet, and which usually contain more than one prose-foot. The term "cadence" should, therefore, be avoided in naming effects due to prose-rhythm.

SINGLE FEET

From the table given in chap. I, it will have been noticed that the range of feet in prose is much greater than in verse. Monosyllabic and dissyllabic feet are common to both poetry and prose, but certain trisyllabics, rarely or never present in verse, are to be found in prose. These are the amphibrach ×′× (called by Mr Bridges "the britannic"), bacchius ′′×, anti-bacchius ×′′, cretic ′×′, and molossus ′′′. The molossus is rare, and the occurrence of the tribrach (× × ×) is doubtful owing to the tendency for secondary stress to occur in a series of three or more light syllables.[3] In ordinary prose, feet of any kind possessing more than one strong stress are rare; feet such as those just mentioned (with the exception of the amphibrach) are more frequent in "numerous" or highly rhythmical prose.

---

[1] "English Prose Numbers". The importance of this extract accounts for its repetition here. See p. 27.

[2] See below, p. 74–5.   [3] See above, chap. I, p. 17.

As prose becomes more "numerous" and symphonic
the number of longer feet also increases; feet which
many critics deny to verse. These are paeons (four-
syllable feet) and dochmiacs (five-syllable feet). Sometimes there occur blocks of six or more syllables which
do not definitely split up into smaller groups, and which
may, in less strictly rhythmed prose, assume the position
of feet. Many of the accents in the following passage
are uncertain:

Who are those that are travelling in it and whither are they
going?[1]

Certain words, such as "impenetrability" and Professor
Elton's example, "extraterritoriality", are ugly and
difficult to adapt to any rhythm. Groups such as these,
however, which hold together loosely and whose rhythm
is uncertain, occur chiefly in less rhythmical prose;
prose of a higher kind usually showing a marked
tendency to scan itself.

Before going further the student should satisfy himself that he knows the names of the different feet, and
can recognise them when they occur. For this purpose
he should study the table in chap. I. The following
sentence provides varied material:

But if mán | did pérish | in his fólly | and his síns, | there is
indéed | cáuse | to móurn, | but nó hópes | of béing | cómforted; |
for he shall néver | retúrn | to líght, | or to hópes | of réstitútion: |
thérefore, | bewáre | lest thóu | álso | cóme | into the sáme pláce

[1] W. N. P. Barbellion, "Crying for the Moon", in *Enjoying Life
and other Literary Remains*, p. 33 (London, 1926).

of tórment; | and lét | thy gríef | sìt dówn, | and rést | upon thy
ówn | túrf, | and wéep | till a shówer | spríngs | from thy éyes |
to héal | the wóunds | of thy spírit; | túrn | thy sórrow | into
cáution, | thy gríef | for hím | that is déad | to thy cáre | for
thysélf | who art alíve, | lest thou díe | and fáll | like óne | of the
fóols | whose lífe | is wórse | than déath, | and their déath | is the
cònsummátion | of áll | infelícities.[1]

There are here 55 feet: five monosyllables, nineteen
iambs, two trochees, one spondee, four amphibrachs,
nine anapaests, one dactyl, one anti-bacchius, four fourth
paeons, four third paeons, four dochmiacs, and one group
of six syllables "is the consummation". The student will
do well to practise analysis in this way, noticing the
effects and uses of the different feet, and comparing the
practices of different authors.

Monosyllables

The monosyllable is one of the characteristics of
English as compared with the classical languages, Greek
and Latin, and is used chiefly for emphasis. True
monosyllables seldom lose any of the strength which is
their most noticeable characteristic, no matter what
other feet surround them. There are, however, other
less emphatic, and less detached, "quasi-monosyllables",
which tend to combine with some other foot near by, the
magnet with the most powerful attraction for them
being, probably, the amphibrach ($\times\prime\times$), the combination

---

[1] Jeremy Taylor, in *Anthology of Imaginative Prose*, p. 136 (ed. R. P.
Cowl).

resulting in a di-iamb ($\times$ / $\times$ /). The instability of the di-
iamb has already been noticed, and the reason for its
breaking up into amphibrach and monosyllable rather
than two iambs, as might be expected, lies chiefly in
the difficulty of suppressing the individuality of the
monosyllable in the formation of a longer foot. The
situation is indeed peculiar. Unless joined by a hyphen,
two iambic words do not commonly tend to coalesce to
form a di-iamb; the coalition is usually between amphibrach and monosyllable, but, as soon as it is effected,
the monosyllable tends to break away. The juxtaposition
of several monosyllables tends to lessen the "sledge-
hammer" effect of any one of them, as in the opening
of the celebrated finale of *Hydriotaphia*,

Now since these dead bones,

which, for this very reason, has been scanned in various
ways.

When a monosyllable occurs alone amongst a number
of other feet its effect is striking, as in this example:

I cóuld not | in cóld blóod, | nor excépt | upòn : the impérious |
cáll | of dúty, | attémpt | what I have sét | mysélf | to dó.[1]

In this position a monosyllable has special emphasis
which is best carried by a word possessing a full, rich
sound.

Fullness of sound is also valuable because monosyllables not only arrest attention by emphasis but also
retard the movement of the sentence, thus causing the

[1] J. H. Newman, *Apologia pro Vita Sua*, p. 192 (Oxford, 1913).

attention of the reader to linger over them. Their effect is often heightened when they are immediately preceded, or followed, or both preceded and followed, by a strongly stressed syllable. Thus, in this sentence,

No one ever told a story half so well, nor sò wéll | knéw | what was capable of being told by the pencil,[1]

the monosyllable " knew" follows a strongly stressed syllable.

Emphasis is further increased when a monosyllable is followed by a pause. In the following example the monosyllable is not only followed by, but also follows, a pause, and is thus completely isolated:

I will not, Francesco! | nó, | I may not commemorate the incidents she related me....[2]

Professor Saintsbury notices[3] that a monosyllable is sometimes used to close a paragraph, as in the following paragraph-ending from Carlyle:

Dark is the way of the Eternal as mirrored in this world of Time: God's way is in the sea, and His path in the gréat | déep.[4]

Owing, however, to their emphatic nature, monosyllables need to be handled with special care. Their too frequent use produces a jerky and halting style, a defect which is very apparent in the writings of Carlyle.

---

[1] Hazlitt, ''On a Landscape of Nicolas Poussin", in *Table Talk* (*Works*, ed. Waller and Glover, vi, p. 171, London, 1903).

[2] *Selections from Landor*, p. 170 (ed. Sidney Colvin, London, 1902).

[3] *History of Prose Rhythm*, p. 89. See also chap. iii, below, p. 83.

[4] *The French Revolution*, Part II, Bk i, chap. i, closing paragraph.

Dissyllabic and trisyllabic feet

Little need be said about these, the staple feet of
ordinary prose. It has already been noticed that some
trisyllabics, rarely or never present in verse, are to
be found in prose. Unlike monosyllables, which are
characteristically emphatic, other feet cannot be described as producing certain effects, because they are
constantly modified by the feet around them. The
special effects produced by position in this way will be
noticed as they occur.

Many English rhythms are trochaic, but the staple
feet of ordinary conversation and conversational prose
are iambs, amphibrachs, and anapaests, as the following
example will show:

You should háve | both ápples | and núts | in the hóuse. |
You pút | the ápples | in a wáter-túb | and dúck : for thèm. |
And you tíe them | to stícks, | which are máde | to twírl : róund |
rápidly. | Your jób | is to snátch | an ápple | with your téeth, |
and withóut | úsing | your hánds | to hélp you.   (Daily paper.)

Though seldom, some prosodists say never, present in
verse, the amphibrach is very common in prose. The
frequency of its occurrence is noticeable in the following
instance:

The véry | lánguage | of Gíbbon | shóws | these quálities. |
Its majéstic | márch | has béen | the àdmirátion, | its ráther |
pómpous | cádence | the spórt, | of áll | perúsers.[1]

---

[1] W. Bagehot, *Edward Gibbon* (*Works of Bagehot*, ed. Barrington,
p. 160, London, 1915).

Attention may be called to the juxtaposition of amphi-
brach and monosyllable in "of Gíbbon | shóws", but
here there is no combination.

The amphibrach is even more prominent in this
sentence:

Nóthing | sublímely | artístic | has éver | arísen | out of
mére | árt.[1]

The anapaest is also common in prose but if used too
frequently its peculiarly lilting movement soon tends to
become over-suggestive of metre, as, for instance, in the
following sequence:

...in a vóice | that seemed frésh | as the plásh | of a láugh |
in the dárk | from a bóat | coming hóme.[2]

Feet of more than three syllables

Paeons are found in abundance in rhythmical or
"numerous" prose. Aristotle himself, as we have
noticed,[3] commented on their value in the prose of his
own time. Of the different types of paeon, many English
writers of highly rhythmical prose show a marked
preference for the third paeon ($\times\times\diagup\times$), perhaps because
of its tendency, noticed by Professor Saintsbury, to set
up an "ionic a minore" movement which is usually
very effective. "But for the more ornate and numerous
prose...the *third* paeon, especially when, by the

[1] G. K. Chesterton, "A Defence of Nonsense", in *Modern English
Essays*, IV, p. 229 (ed. Ernest Rhys, London, 1922).

[2] C. E. Montague, *The Morning's War*, p. 29 (London, 1913).

[3] Chap. I, p. 24.

large commonness of English, the final syllable manu-
factures something like an Ionic *a minore,* is found and
found in a great, perhaps a predominant, portion of
those passages which aim at special harmonic effect".[1]

There are several third paeons in this sentence from
Gibbon:

But the júrisprúdence | of the Pándects | is círcumscríbed |
withín | a périod | of a húndred | yéars, | from the pèrpétual |
édict | to the déath | of Sevérus | Àlexánder; | the civílians |
who líved | under the fírst | Cáesars | are séldom | permítted |
to spéak, | and ónly | thrée námes | can be attríbuted | to the
áge | of the repúblic.[2]

The following sentence from Oscar Wilde abounds in
paeons:

Déar to him | was the pérfume | of the béan fíeld | at évening, |
and déar to him | the ódorous | éared-spíkenàrd | that gréw | on
the Sýrian | híIls, | and the frésh : gréen : thýme, | the wíne-
cúp's | chárm.[3]

English, and especially the Anglo-Saxon element of it,
is noticeably monosyllabic and dissyllabic in character,
so that paeons are the most abundant whenever the
diction shows frequent borrowings from those foreign
languages, such as Latin, which are naturally polysyl-
labic. This explains why the broad, sweeping paeonic
movement is prominent in so many of the ornate writings

[1] *History of Prose Rhythm,* p. 452.

[2] Gibbon, *Decline and Fall of the Roman Empire (English Prose
Selections,* ed. Sir Hy. Craik, IV, p. 467, London, 1890–6).

[3] *Anthology of Imaginative Prose,* p. 305 (ed. R. P. Cowl).

of the seventeenth century, a time when the influx of
Latin words into English prose was great, and why
meditative, philosophical, and religious prose tends to
fall into these complex movements. In the following
sentence the short feet of the last section, which is
composed mainly of Saxon words, contrast notably with
the " largeness " of the remainder :

And if ány | have beèn so háppy | as trúly | to ùnderstánd |
Chrístian | anníhilátion, | éxtasis, | éxolútion, | lìquefáction, |
tránsformátion, | the kíss of the Spóuse, | gùstátion of Gód, |
and ingréssion | into the divíne | shádow, | thèy : have alréady |
had an hándsome | ànticipátion | of héaven ; | the glóry | of the
wórld | is súrely | óver, | and the éarth | in áshes | únto thèm.[1]

The prominence of amphibrach and anapaest among
these short feet is also marked.

Before passing from the consideration of individual
feet to their combinations and the rhythm of sentence
and paragraph, several general rhythmical features
must be noticed. In the preceding chapter[2] it was
shown that, unlike that of metre, the rhythm of prose
does not depend upon fidelity to a fixed pattern, but on
the combined satisfaction and disappointment of the
sense of pattern. Thus it was concluded that variety is
an important principle of prose-rhythm ; since the mind
is to organise the materials into some order which it
can perceive as being rhythmical, it must be assisted by

[1] Sir T. Browne, *Hydriotaphia*, chap. v (*Works*, ed. Wilkin-Bohn,
iii, pp. 48, 49, 1852).
[2] Chap. i, p. 14 *et seq*.

the presence of some degree of recurrence. Thus, it may be stated that *both recurrence and variety are essential ingredients of rhythmical prose.* This sentence is the key to our subject.

An examination of highly rhythmical prose, such as that of Sir Thomas Browne, or Jeremy Taylor, or De Quincey, or Pater, or, indeed, of almost any of the great "diploma-pieces", shows considerable care on the part of the writer in obtaining variety by avoiding successions of the same feet. Thus, in the following extract from Pater, only once do two feet of the same kind occur together, and never more than two:

So the chíld | of whóm | I am wríting | líved ón there | quíetly; | thíngs : withóut | thus mínistering | tó him, | as he sát | dáily | at the wíndow | with the bírdcáge | hánging | belów it, | and his móther | táught him | to réad, | wóndering | at the éase | with whích | he léarned, | and at the quíckness | of his mémory. | The pérfume | of the líttle | flówers | of the líme-trée | féll | through the áir | upón them | like ráin; | while tíme | séemed | to móve | éver | móre slówly | to the múrmur | of the bées in it, | till it álmost | stóod stíll | on Júne | áfternóons.[1]

The use of long feet such as paeons and dochmiacs is a great aid to variety. The number of different feet of four or more syllables is enormous compared with the number of feet of two or three. Moreover, as Professor Saintsbury says, prose "is more tolerant of repeated identical tetrasyllabic feet than of shorter ones".[2] Thus,

[1] Pater, "The Child in the House", in *Miscellaneous Studies*, p. 177 (London, 1907).

[2] *History of Prose Rhythm*, p. 139.

considerable skill is required to prevent similarity, and consequent tendency towards metre, in sequences of dissyllabic and trisyllabic feet. The following is skilfully varied:

In a féw | yéars | máss | is sáid | in St Pául's; | mátins | and véspers | are súng | in Yórk : Mínster....[1]

But whenever sequences of short feet are attempted there is grave danger of falling into blank verse. In the following examples recurrence is so obvious and insistent as to be metrical:

...in sígn | whereóf | they háng | the déad | séa-bírd | róund | his néck.[2]

If Coleridge had written "around" instead of "round", the recurrence would have been still more noticeable. Similarly, a sentence in Professor Bradley's *Shakespearean Tragedy* splits up into closely correspondent halves:

Her chíef anxíety appéars to bé
that he shóuld not betráy his mísery.[3]

Correspondence is here further emphasised by the approximation to rhyme in "be" and "misery".

Regularity of movement, however, is permissible, and may greatly enhance the beauty of the rhythm, when prose-rhythm cannot be mistaken for metre. According to Professor Saintsbury: "Verses or parts of verses, which present themselves to the ear as such, are strictly to be avoided in prose; but such as break themselves into

[1] Thackeray, *The Four Georges, George the First.*
[2] Coleridge, Prose commentary to the *Ancient Mariner.*
[3] A. C. Bradley, *Shakespearean Tragedy*, p. 375 (London, 1904).

prose adjustments are permissible, and even strengthen
and sweeten the 'numerous' character very much".[1]
Thus, it would be unwise to condemn this passage,
because, by disregarding the prose-foot divisions, it can
be represented as metrical or at any rate quasi-metrical:

The chóruses | swéep | down the wínd, | tírelessly, | flíght |
after flíght, | till the bréathless | sóul | almost críes | for respíte |
from the unrólling | spléndours.[2]

Although recurrence is marked, the rhythm of this
sentence remains proper to prose.

Variety is frequently obtained by varying simple
rhythms composed chiefly of dissyllabic and trisyllabic
feet with complex paeonic movements. The following is
an example of simple rhythm:

And thése | were the fírst | róse-trées | and róses, | both
whíte | and réd, | that éver | àny mán | sáw; | and thús | was
thís | máiden | sáved | by the gráce | of Gód. | And thérefore |
is that fíeld | clépt | the fíeld | of Gód | flóurished, | for it was
fúll | of róses.[3]

A striking contrast to this simple movement is afforded
by the complex rhythm of the following sentence from
Burke:

This wáy | of proscríbing | the cítizens | by denóminátions |
and géneral | descríptions, | dígnified | by the náme | of réason |
of státe, | and secúrity | for constitútions | and cómmonwéalths, |
is nóthing | bétter, | at bóttom, | than the míserable | invéntion |

[1] *History of Prose Rhythm*, p. 480.

[2] Francis Thompson, *Shelley*, p. 59 (London, 1909).

[3] Sir John Mandeville, in *Anthology of Imaginative Prose*, p. 2
(ed. R. P. Cowl).

of an ungénerous | ambítion, | which would fáin : hòld : the
sácred | trúst | of pówer, | without ány | of the vírtues | or ány |
of the énergies | that give a títle to it; | a recéipt | of pólicy, |
made úp | of a detéstable | cómpound | of málice, | cówardice, |
and slóth.

Both types of rhythm are frequently to be found in
the same paragraph, and sometimes in the same sentence,
as, for instance, in that quoted above on p. 44.

Closely connected with this is the use of synonymous
words and phrases, a practice which is especially pre-
valent in rhetorical prose. Sometimes a Latin phrase is
followed by its English equivalent and an effective
contrast in sound and rhythm thus secured, but more
frequently all the words are English. The coupling of
synonymous or almost synonymous words such as "give
and bestow" is a device possessing enormous rhythmical
possibilities, possibilities which were first shown by the
fifteenth-century prose writers, and developed later in
the magnificence of the *Authorised Version of the Bible*.

Rising and *waved* rhythms are the basic rhythms of
English speech. *Falling* and *level* rhythms are comparatively rare and their use, therefore, often provides
variety. Especially effective is the introduction of trochee
or dactyl into a passage of *rising* or *waved* rhythm. Both
variety and emphasis are obtained and the movement of
the sentence arrested or held up, as in this example :

But the iníquity | of oblívion | blíndly | scáttereth | her
póppy.[1]

[1] Sir Thomas Browne, *Hydriotaphia*, chap. v (*Works*, ed. Wilkin-
Bohn, iii, p. 44, 1852).

This sentence also provides an example of another device common to many writers of rhythmical prose. This is the choice of " -eth " instead of " -s ", as the ending of the third person singular of the present indicative; a choice useful in obtaining variety or avoiding a succession of sibilants. In the seventeenth century these alternative endings were used with almost equal frequency, the preference for one form or the other in particular places being guided by the need for variety in sound and rhythm. The following is an example from Donne:

> One *dieth* at his full strength, being wholly at ease, and in quiet, and another *dies* in the bitterness of his soul, and never eats with pleasure; but they lie down alike in the dust, and the worm covers them.[1]

Another adjustment made to ensure ease of movement is exemplified in this sentence:

> O Lord, rebuke me not in *thine* anger, neither chasten me in *thy* hot displeasure.[2]

This sentence also makes use of a device which is especially common in rhetorical prose and is frequently used for its binding effect. This is the use of synonymous, or almost synonymous, phrases in apposition as in "rebuke me not in thine anger" and "neither chasten me in thy hot displeasure". The rhythm of the *Authorised Version* owes not a little to this device.

---

[1] *English Prose Selections*, II, p. 91 (ed. Sir Hy. Craik).
[2] *Authorised Version of the Bible*, Psalm vi.

SENTENCE-RHYTHM

"In fully developed prose-rhythm", writes Professor Saintsbury, "'a beginning, a middle, and an end' are to be demanded and respected as impartially as in an Aristotelian tragedy".[1] It is of no use to begin well and continue badly, or to begin badly and end well. The excellence of beginning or middle or end will not make up for defects in the other two. It was the great fault of writers such as Milton and Clarendon that they often ended badly; after a good beginning their sentences frequently became too involved and dragged on too long.[2] The changes in sentence-rhythm from time to time are described by Professor Saintsbury in these words:

It was the fault of the early stages that they did not take care either of beginning, or middle, or end; it was the virtue of the great sixteenth- or seventeenth-century writers that they took equal care of all; the fault of the succeeding school that these "middles" were specially neglected; and the glory of the nineteenth-century restorers, from Coleridge onwards, that they minded them.[3]

Beginning

Seldom in English prose do sentences begin with a strong stress. The emphatic opening is not for all work in English. It may amuse the reader to count the number of sentences beginning with a strong stress in any passage of ordinary prose which he may be reading. He will find some; and of these the majority will probably

[1] *History of Prose Rhythm*, p. 458.   [2] See below, p. 61.
[3] *History of Prose Rhythm*, p. 459.

begin with a foot such as a trochee, dactyl, first paeon,
or spondee. Monosyllabic openings are still more emphatic and are very rare. Carlyle constantly makes use
of monosyllabic and strongly stressed openings, but his
practice is the exception rather than the rule. The
following is a typical passage from *Sartor Resartus*:

Póor, | wandering, wayward man! Àrt thou not tíred, | and
beaten with stripes, even as I am? Éver, | whether thou bear
the royal mantle or the beggar's gaberdine, art thou not so
weary, so heavy-laden; and thy Bed of Rest is but a Grave.
Ó | my brother, my brother, why cannot I shelter thee in my
bosom, and wipe away all tears from thy eyes! Trúly, | the din
of many-voiced Life, which, in this solitude with the mind's
organ I could hear, was no longer maddening discord but a
melting one; like inarticulate cries, and sobbings of a dumb
creature, which in the ear of Heaven are prayers.[1]

There are five sentences here, four of which begin
with a strong, and one with a secondary, stress.

   1. Póor |....   2. Àrt thou not tíred |....   3. Éver |....
               4. Ó |....   5. Trúly | ....

It will be noticed that two of these openings are monosyllabic. Carlyle's style is, indeed, notoriously heavy.
Other writers have an easier, more flowing, manner with
a smaller percentage of strong stresses.

English prose sentences usually begin with a weak
syllable, and the iamb seems to be a particularly
favoured foot. A favourite device of the writers of
"numerous" prose is to work up from an iambic

---

[1] Carlyle, *Sartor Resartus*, Bk II, chap. IX (*Works*, I, pp. 150-1,
London, 1896).

beginning through one of an infinite variety of combinations to a climax or carefully wrought "middle". Here
are three much-quoted sentences from the book of Isaiah,
each beginning with an iamb and all proceeding thence
by way of different adjustments:

Aríse, | shíne; | for thy líght | is cóme, | and the glóry | of the
Lórd | is rísen | upón thee.

The sún | shall bè no móre | thy líght | by dáy; | néither |
for bríghtness | shall the móon | give líght : ùnto thee: | but the
Lórd | shall bé unto thee | an èverlásting | líght, | and thy Gód |
thy glóry.

Thy sún | shall no móre | go dówn; | néither | shall thy móon |
withdráw itself: | for the Lórd | shall bè : thine èverlásting |
líght, | and the dáys | of thy móurning | shall be énded.[1]

In the first of these the climax is reached almost
immediately. It is a loud, clear, call to be joyful, as
clear in its simplicity as the "light" which "is come".
"Aríse, | shíne; | for thy light is come". The second and
the third sentences are more complex variations of the
theme of the first. They are strangely similar and
different:

2. The sún | shall bè no móre |
    thy líght | by dáy;
néither | for bríghtness | shall the
    móon | give líght : ùnto thee:
but the Lórd | shall bé unto thee |
    an èverlásting | líght,
and thy Gód | thy glóry.

3. Thy sún | shall no móre |
    go dówn;
néither | shall thy móon |
    withdráw itself:
for the Lórd | shall bè : thine
    èverlásting | líght,
and the dáys | of thy móurning |
    shall be énded.

[1] *Authorised Version*, Isaiah, chap. lx.

The constant flashing forth, as it were, of the word "light" is to be noticed throughout.

Middle

Care of the beginning and end of a sentence is not sufficient for rhythmical prose. As Professor Saintsbury points out: "Neglect of the middle will infallibly deprive the structure of all claim to be really 'numerous'. A mere 'filling' of undistinguished rhythm, between an emphatic beginning and end, is French rather than English, oratorical rather than literary, and always indicative of a low type with us".[1] There are many ways of building these "middles", and even if it were possible to tabulate them all, it would be of little value. The function of this (or any study of prose-rhythm) should not be to attempt to give a recipe for the production of "numerous" prose, for this would be attempting the impossible, but to point out some of the practices by which great masters achieved their effects.[2]

A much-favoured "middle" is that built up of a series of lengthening and shortening feet carefully arranged. Sometimes the number of syllables in each foot increases towards the middle of the clause or sentence, and then decreases, as in this example from Milton:

[1] *History of Prose Rhythm*, p. 479.

[2] There is no suggestion here, or elsewhere in this book, that the great masters of rhythmical prose *consciously* used certain feet, or combinations of feet, to produce particular effects. This question can have no place here.

Trúth | indéed | càme ónce | into the wórld | with her divíne | máster.[1]

Here the numbers of syllables in successive feet are 1.2.2.4.4.2.

Sometimes the number of syllables in each foot decreases towards the middle and then increases, as in this example:

But his énemies | had pássed | the níght | in équal | disórder | and anxíety.[2]

The sequence here is 5.2.2.3.3.5.

There is a quality of unexpectedness when a short foot follows a series of lengthening feet. The gradual increase in the number of syllables in each successive foot leads the reader to expect a long foot as the apex of the clause, and a short foot thus gives a pleasurable surprise. The following extract from Coleridge teems with examples of this, which the student will do well to notice for himself:

A drizzling rain. Heavy masses of shapeless vapour upon the mountains (O the perpetual forms of Borrowdale!) yet it is no unbroken tale of dull sadness. Slanting pillars travel across the lake at long intervals; the vaporous mass whitens in large stains of light—on the lakeward ridge of that huge arm-chair of Lodore fell a gleam of softest light, that brought out the rich hues of late autumn. The woody Castle Crag between me and Lodore is a rich flower garden of colours—the brightest yellows with the

---

[1] Milton, *Areopagitica* (*Prose Works*, ed. Bohn, II, p. 89, 1901).

[2] Gibbon, *Decline and Fall of the Roman Empire* (*English Prose Selections*, ed. Sir Hy. Craik, IV, p. 464).

deepest crimsons and the infinite shades of brown and green, the infinite diversity of which blends the whole, so that the brighter colours seem to be colours upon a ground, not coloured things.[1]

This step-like arrangement of feet, Professor Saintsbury terms "gradation", and, as we have seen, gradation may be either way; the number of syllables in successive feet may either increase or diminish.

Sometimes gradation goes the same way in successive sequences of feet. In the following sentence gradation in each phrase is from short to long:

Só | when thís | corrúptible | shall have pút ón | incorrúption, (1.2.4.4.4)
and thís | mórtal | shall have pút ón | immortálity, (2.2.4.5)
thén | shall be bróught | to páss | the sáying | that is wrítten,
(1.3.2.3.4)
Déath | is swállowed ùp | in víctory.[2] (1.4.4)

Juxtaposition of strong stresses, with or without gradation, forms an effective climax, or "arch", as Professor Saintsbury calls it, to the sentence. The movement is arrested and the attention of the reader held for a moment, as in this example:

Why do we bathe our limbs in swéet wáters, and embalm our bodies with rích pérfumes, when nó cárrion in the world can smell more noisome than must our carcases?[3]

Mr van Draat asserts that "The first and essential con-

[1] Coleridge, *Anima Poetae* (October 21, 1803), p. 34, London, 1895.
[2] First Epistle to the Corinthians, chap. xv.
[3] Thomas Dekker, in *Anthology of Imaginative Prose*, pp. 34–5 (ed. R. P. Cowl).

dition for the securing of rhythmical movement is the avoidance of two strest syllables in immediate succession",[1] but the clashing of strong stress can be very effective as it is in the sentence just quoted, and in the following:

This áire-: encírcled | Glóbe | is the sóle | Région | of Déath....[2]

Indeed, in view of the effective use of consecutive strong stresses made by writers of "numerous" prose, Mr van Draat's assertion seems difficult to support.

Another useful and much-favoured sentence pivot is the monosyllable, as the following examples will show:

Entering among them, a fresher savour and a larger | breath | strikes one upon the lips and forehead.[3]

But many are too early | old | and before the date of age.[4]

The fullness of sound of the monosyllable is very noticeable in the latter quotation.

Monosyllables sometimes appear to be in apposition to each other, and rear themselves up, as it were, from the undulation of the sentence, as in the following instance:

To the absolute beauty of its artistic | form | is added the accidental, tranquil, | charm | of familiarity.[5]

[1] P. Fijn van Draat, *Rhythm in English Prose*, p. 9. See above, p. 31.

[2] Wm. Drummond, *A Cypresse Grove* (*Poetical Works*, ed. L. E. Kastner, ii, p. 71, Manchester Univ. Press, 1913).

[3] Swinburne, *Blake*, p. 127 (London, 1906).

[4] Sir Thomas Browne, *Hydriotaphia*, chap. v (*Works*, ed. Wilkin-Bohn, iii, p. 42, 1852).

[5] Walter Pater, *Appreciations*, p. 245 (London, 1904).

In many sentences there is no definite pivot; the rhythm is undulating, rising and falling with a gentle motion, as in this example:

The bróad : móon | língers | on the súmmit | of Móunt | Ólivet, | but its béam | has lóng | left the gárden | of Gethsémane | and the tómb | of Ábsalom, | the wáters | of Kédron | and the dárk | abýss | of Jehósaphát.[1]

Sometimes the middle is a long foot such as the dochmiac; combinations of feet are frequently "geared on", as Professor Saintsbury says, in this way. In the following example the dochmiac which follows the semicolon also helps to preserve the rhythmical continuity of the sentence:

The dáy | begíns | agáin ; | and how wónderful | is the retúrn | of the dáy, | híll after híll | rísing óut | of the shádow.[2]

In a balanced style the middles are often composed of similar rhythm-groups or clauses carefully balanced or alternated. The prose of Johnson affords many examples of this feature which will be discussed below.[3]

End

The rhythmical importance of the end of a sentence, and to a lesser degree, of clause or phrase, has long been recognised. Writers of ancient Greece and Rome made use in their endings of certain rhythmical sequences,

[1] Lord Beaconsfield, in *Anthology of Imaginative Prose*, p. 245 (ed. R. P. Cowl).

[2] George Moore, *The Brook Kerith*, p. 291 (London, 1927).

[3] See p. 69.

chosen for their effect, called *cursus*, and equivalents of
these are to be found in English "numerous" prose to
this day. According to plan, however, this chapter is
concerned with strictly "prose-rhythmical" effects and
cadence will be reserved for the next.

Gradation again plays an important part in the construction of endings. Gradation downwards from long
feet to short seems to be specially frequent and effective.
This dropping-off, as it were, of syllables from foot to
foot towards the close of a sentence may be illustrated
by the following:

Thát géntleman | would dríve | his fríend | Ríchmond, | the
bláck | bóxer, | down to Móulsey, | and hóld | his cóat, | and
shóut | and swéar, | and hurráh | with delíght | whilst the bláck
mán | was béating | Dútch Sám, | the Jéw.[1]

The sense here is continuous, and rhythmical continuity is maintained by avoiding gradation until the
end of the sentence is reached. Sometimes gradation
begins at some distance from the end, on the type
6.5.4.3.2 (the numbers as usual denoting the number
of syllables in each foot), though it is seldom to be found
so exact as this. The following ending drops suddenly
from a foot of six syllables to one of three:

...to wítnesse | and recóunt | the wórthy | achíevements |
of their invíncible | and dréadfull | Návy.[2]

[1] Thackeray, *The Four Georges. George the Fourth*, p. 120 (Collins,
London).

[2] Raleigh, *Last Fight of the Revenge*, p. 16 (Arber's Reprint, 1901).

For obvious reasons gradation from short feet to long is not nearly so effective at the end of a sentence. The "dying away" effect of decreasing length of feet is much more suitable at the end.

Recession or advance of strong stress in consecutive feet towards the end of a sentence is frequently found. The following sequences will explain what is meant:

(a) ′× × × | ×′× × | × ×′× | × × ×′; showing recession of strong stress (the accented syllable recedes further towards the end of the foot in each consecutive foot), for example:

ceremonies | of bravery | in the infamy | of his nature.[1]

(b) × × ×′ | × ×′× | ×′× × | ′× × ×; showing advance of strong stress (the accented syllable advances towards the beginning of the foot in each successive foot), for example:

emblems | and coruscations | of invisible | unoriginate | perfection.[2]

Professor Saintsbury states that the "most beautiful endings in English are trochaic or quasi-trochaic".[3] Yet, though no one would question the beauty of this type of ending in which the sound gradually dies away with a melancholy sweetness, it is a little hazardous to say

[1] Sir T. Browne, *Hydriotaphia*, chap. v (*Works*, ed. Wilkin-Bohn, iii, p. 47, 1852).

[2] Cardinal Newman, in *Anthology of Imaginative Prose*, p. 252 (ed. R. P. Cowl).

[3] *History of Prose Rhythm*, p. 458.

that it is the "most beautiful" English ending. It may be noticed, in passing, that many of these trochaic endings which are considered by Professor Saintsbury to be specially effective correspond in some measure to the classical *cursus* (see chap. III), although Professor Saintsbury doubts the existence, in English prose, of endings analogous to the *cursus*.

In giving first place, however, to the trochaic ending, he does not decry the stronger iambic; "the abrupter iambic or quasi-iambic close has a strength and weight of its own, and an admixture of the two is undoubtedly desirable in the formation of a perfect paragraph...".[1] From the next chapter it will be seen that this admixture is present in most "numerous" prose. The comparative beauty of iambic and trochaic endings matters little; far more important is the consideration of their suitability to the rhythm and subject-matter of their context.

Little more will be said here concerning clause- and sentence-ends. Discussion of their chief features belongs to the next chapter, but from the foregoing remarks two general principles have emerged.

The first of these is that the ends of clauses or sentences should not be too closely correspondent in prose-rhythm or they will tend either to become metrical or to give the effect of mechanical and monotonous balance. This last word, gives its name to prose, such as that of Johnson, of which it is the most striking feature, and

[1] *History of Prose Rhythm*, p. 458.

examples of this "balanced" prose will be found below.
It is also, for obvious reasons, much easier to find examples
of almost metrical correspondence in highly balanced
prose than in prose whose rhythm is more continuous,
but even here examples are occasionally to be found.
The following is an instance:

But who knows the fate of his bones, | or how óften | hè is |
to be búried?

Who hath the oracle of his ashes, | or whíther | thèy are | to
be scáttered?[1]

The final clauses of these two sentences are almost
identical in rhythm:

$$\times \times \prime \times \mid \prime \times \mid \times \times \prime \times,$$
$$\times \prime \times \mid \prime \times \mid \times \times \prime \times.$$

The second principle seems to be that care should
always be taken not to conduct the rhythm to an effective
close before the end of the clause or sentence is reached.
Disregard of this was the great fault of those seventeenth-century writers, such as Milton and Clarendon,
who frequently bring a sentence to a dying close and
then, as Professor Saintsbury says, "kick it up" with an
unexpected appendix. The following sentence labours
and flounders unsteadily in this way:

To come within the narrowness of household government,
observation will show us many deep counsellors of state and
judges to demean themselves incorruptly in the settled course

[1] Sir T. Browne, *Hydriotaphia, Epistle Dedicatory* (*Works*, ed.
Wilkin-Bohn, III, p. 3, 1852).

of affairs, and many worthy preachers upright in their lives, powerful in their audience: but look upon either of these men where they are left to their own disciplining at home, and you shall soon perceive, for all their single knowledge and uprightness, how deficient they are in the regulating of their own family; not only in what may concern the virtuous and decent composure of their minds in their several places, but, that which is of a lower and easier performance, the right possessing of the outward vessel, their body, in health or sickness, rest or labour, diet or abstinence, whereby to render it more pliant to the soul, and useful to the commonwealth: which if men were but as good to discipline themselves, as some are to tutor their horses and hawks, it could not be so gross in most households.[1]

PARAGRAPH-RHYTHM

Owing to the "looseness" of the movement of prose compared with that of verse, it is far more difficult to discuss the rhythm of a prose-paragraph than that of a stanza or even a verse-paragraph such as those of Milton. The psychological difficulty which hampers all discussion of prose-rhythm is here particularly forbidding. Systematic satisfaction of rhythmical expectancy is much easier to comprehend than the complicated mass of satisfactions and disappointments without any scheme which is the basis of prose-rhythm. There are, however, certain definite practices giving law and order to paragraphs which should not escape notice.

An obvious way of constructing a rhythmically con-

[1] Milton, *The Reason of Church Government* (*Prose Works*, ed. Bohn, ii, p. 443, 1901).

nected paragraph is by the use of a theme which is repeated from time to time with or without slight variations. The theme may consist of a single word such as "law" as in this passage:

This world's first creation, and the preservation since of things created, what is it but only so far forth a manifestation by execution, what the eternal *law* of God is concerning things natural? And as it cometh to pass in a kingdom rightly ordered, that after a *law* is once published, it presently takes effect far and wide, all states framing themselves thereunto; even so let us think it fareth in the natural course of the world: since the time that God did first proclaim the edicts of His *law* upon it, heaven and earth have hearkened unto His voice, and their labour hath been to do His will. "He made a *law* for the rain"; He gave His "decree unto the sea, that the waters should not pass His commandment". Now if nature should intermit her course and leave altogether, though it were but for a while, the observation of her own *laws*; if those principal and mother elements of the world, whereof all things in this world are made, should lose the qualities which now they have; if the frame of that heavenly arch erected over our heads should loosen and dissolve itself; if celestial spheres should forget their wonted motions, and by irregular volubility turn themselves any way as it might happen; if the prince of the light of heaven, which now as a giant doth run his unwearied course, should as it were with a languishing faintness, begin to stand and to rest himself; if the moon should wander from her beaten way, the times and seasons of the year blend themselves by disordered and confused mixture, the winds breathe out their last gasp, the clouds yield no rain, the earth be defeated of heavenly influence, the fruits of the earth pine away as children at the withered breasts of their mother no longer able to yield them relief; what would become of man himself, whom these things now do all serve? See we not plainly, that obedience of creatures unto the *law* of nature is the stay of the whole world?[1]

The finality and binding effect of the last "law" after the long and impassioned sentence preceding it, one of Hooker's best-known "purple patches", is especially noticeable.

When used too frequently, repetition can be bad, and, instead of connecting, will break up the paragraph-rhythm, as in this example:

Howling is the noise of hell, singing the voice of *heaven*; sadness the damp of hell, rejoicing the serenity of *heaven*. And he that hath not this joy here, lacks one of the best pieces of his evidence for the joys of *heaven*; and hath neglected or refused that earnest, by which God uses to bind His bargain that true joy in this world shall flow into the joy of *heaven*, as a river flows into the sea; this joy shall not be put out in death, and a new joy kindled in me in *heaven*; but as my soul, as soon as it is out of my body, is in *heaven*, and does not stay for the possession of *heaven*, nor for the fruition of the sight of God, till it be ascended through air, and fire, and moon, and sun, and planets, and firmament, to that place which we conceive to be *heaven*, but without the thousandth part of a minute's stop, as soon as it issues, is in a glorious light, which is *heaven* (for all the way to *heaven* is *heaven*; and as those angels which come from *heaven* hither, bring *heaven* with them, and are in *heaven* here, so that soul that goes to *heaven*, meets *heaven* here; and as those angels do not divest *heaven* by coming, so these souls invest *heaven*, in their going).

[1] Hooker, *Laws of Ecclesiastical Polity*, Bk i, pp. 13–14 (ed. R. W. Church, Oxford, 1905).

As my soul shall not go towards *heaven*, but go by *heaven* to *heaven*, to the *heaven* of *heavens*, so the true joy of a good soul in this world is the very joy of *heaven*. ...[1]

Instead of a single word, the theme may consist of a group of words, as in this passage from Sir Thomas Browne:

This is the day that must make good that great attribute of God, His Justice; that must reconcile those unanswerable doubts that torment the wisest understandings; and reduce those seeming inequalities and respective distributions in this world to an equality and recompensive Justice in the next. *This is that one day*, that shall include and comprehend all that went before it; wherein, as in the last scene, all the Actors must enter, to compleat and make up the Catastrophe of this great piece. *This is the day* whose memory hath only power to make us honest in the dark, and to be virtuous without a witness.[2]

In reading this passage the powerful underhum of "ionic a minore" cannot fail to be noticed throughout.[3] It is a feature of several closely correspondent rhythm-groups:

> day that must make good
> distributions in this world
> This is that one day
> comprehend all
> as in the last scene
> compleat and make up
> of this great piece

[1] John Donne. [2] Sir T. Browne, *Religio Medici*, I, xlvii.
[3] See above, p. 43.

More will be said about groupings of this kind in the next chapter.

Professor Saintsbury condemns, almost without exception, "pivotal arrangements of the same word or words" as being "too rough and boisterous" for higher prose and sinning against Variety.[1] But repetition of either single word or phrase is a feature of oratorical prose and has been employed with a striking effect. Burke's speeches are full of paragraphs founded on some dominant word or words, the recurrence of which gives the keynote of both sense and rhythm. Repetition, or "epanaphora" as it is technically termed, can give law and order to rhythm without making it metrical or otherwise untrue to the nature of good prose. Sometimes it is bad, as in the example from Donne quoted above in which "heaven" is repeated too frequently, or, as in the following example in which repetition of similar phrases is monotonous:

All of us, so far as we are *Barbarians, Philistines*, or *Populace*, imagine happiness to consist in doing *what one's ordinary self likes. What one's ordinary self likes* differs according to the *class* to which one belongs, and has its *severer* and *lighter* side ; always, however, remaining *machinery* and nothing more. *The graver self* of the *Barbarian* likes (honours and consideration) ; *his more relaxed self*, (field sports and pleasure). *The graver self* of *one kind of Philistine* likes fanaticism, business, and money-making ; *his more relaxed self*, comfort and tea-meetings. Of *another kind of Philistine, the graver self* likes rattening; *the relaxed self*, deputations or hearing Mr Odger speak. *The sterner self* of the *Populace*

[1] *History of Prose Rhythm*, p. 463.

likes bawling, hustling and smashing; *the lighter self*, beer. But in each *class* there are born a certain number of natures with a curiosity about their *best self*, with a bent for seeing things as they are, for disentangling themselves from *machinery*, for simply concerning themselves with reason and the will of God, and doing their best to make these prevail;—for the pursuit, in a word, of perfection.[1]

Arnold has a habit of opposing batches of words in this way; a habit which frequently becomes a vice, as in this paragraph.

Paragraphs are often built up of long and short sentences arranged in a manner akin to gradation. This mixture of long and short sentences, recommended by Dionysius, may not be monotonous but, when used too frequently, soon produces a mechanical effect. "Excessive contraction and letting out", writes Professor Saintsbury, "the constant sending forth giant and dwarf in company, communicates the smatch of cheap epigram—the sound and the scent of the halfpenny or farthing cracker".[2] Macaulay frequently sins in this way; the following paragraph will furnish an example. In order to emphasise the contrast, the sentences are arranged under one another, the bracketed number at the end of each one showing the number of syllables contained in the sentence:

The serjeants made proclamation. (8)
Hastings advanced to the bar and bent his knee. (11)

[1] Arnold, *Culture and Anarchy*, pp. 98–9 (London, 1882).
[2] *History of Prose Rhythm*, pp. 460–1.

The culprit was indeed not unworthy of that great presence.
(15)

He had ruled an extensive and populous country, had made laws and treaties, had sent forth armies, had set up and pulled down princes. (32)

And in his high place he had so borne himself, that all had feared him, that most had loved him, and that hatred itself could deny him no title to glory except virtue. (41)

He looked like a great man, and not like a bad man. (12)

A person small and emaciated, yet deriving dignity from a carriage which, while it indicated deference to the court, indicated also habitual self-possession and self-respect, a high and intellectual forehead, a brow pensive, but not gloomy, a mouth of inflexible decision, a face pale and worn, but serene, on which was written, as legibly as under the picture in the Council chamber at Calcutta, Mens aequa in arduis; such was the aspect with which the great Proconsul presented himself to his judges. (141)[1]

The staccato effect of the short sentences is especially noticeable.

This gradation of sentences is particularly marked, as Professor Saintsbury points out, in balanced style in which not only the sentences, but also the rhythm-groups and clauses, are carefully opposed and balanced in length (i.e. in number of syllables), in rhythmical movement, or in number of strong stresses. Johnson's prose is, perhaps, one of the best examples of this style. In the following extract the corresponding groups are arranged under each other:

[1] Macaulay, *Warren Hastings*, pp. 112-13 (ed. Deighton, London, 1893).

He will only please long (who)
by témpering the ácid of sátire
with the súgar of civílity,
and alláying the héat of wít
with the frigídity of húmble chát,
can make the true punch of conversation ;
and as thàt púnch can be drúnk in the gréatest quántity
which has the lárgest propórtion of wáter,
so thàt compánion will be the óftenest wélcome
whose tálk flòws óut with inoffénsive cópiousness,
and unénvied insipídity.[1]

It must not be thought that the parallelism of rhythm-
groups, clauses, or sentences was a product only of the
eighteenth century; it had appeared long before in the
work of men such as Lyly, Ascham and Ben Jonson,
and later, in Sir Thomas Browne's *Christian Morals.*
The examples given here, and anywhere in this book,
are not meant to be characteristic of their period unless
quoted as such; they are chosen solely to illustrate the
particular rhythmical effect which is being discussed.

Although balance is a characteristic, sometimes the
only rhythmical characteristic, of an oratorical or
antithetic style, it is, as Professor Saintsbury says,
"noticeable also in the symphonic and polyphonic style,
where the rhythm is rather continuous than antiphonically arranged".[2] If the continuity of movement is sustained, the corresponding rhythm-groups do not tend

---

[1] S. Johnson, *The Idler*, No. 34, Dec. 9, 1758 (*Works*, VIII, p. 137,
London, 1787).

[2] *History of Prose Rhythm*, p. 480.

of their own accord to drop out and face each other
as they do in the sentence just quoted from Johnson.
The prose of Swinburne furnishes good examples of
balanced, yet continuous, rhythm, of which the following
is one:

These at a first naming recall only that incomparable charm
of form in which they first came out clothed, and hence vex the
souls of men with regretful comparison. For here by hard
necessity we miss the lovely and luminous setting of designs,
which makes the "Songs" precious and pleasureable to those who
know or care for little else of the master's doing; the infinite
delight of those drawings, sweeter to see than music to hear,
where herb and stem break into grace of shape and blossom of
form, and the branch-work is full of little flames and flowers,
catching as it were from the verse enclosed the fragrant heat
and delicate sound they seem to give back; where colour lapses
into light and light assumes feature in colour. If elsewhere the
artist's strange strength of thought and hand is more visible,
nowhere is there such pure sweetness and singleness of design in
his work. All the tremulous and tender splendour of Spring is
mixed into the written word and coloured draught; every page
has the smell of April. Over all things given, the sleep of flocks
and the growth of leaves, the laughter in dividing lips of flowers
and the music at the moulded mouth of the flute-player, there
is cast a pure fine veil of light, softer than sleep and keener than
sunshine.[1]

Little search is needed to find balance here, yet the
flow is unbroken, the whole being bound together by a
continuous rhythmical thread.

[1] Swinburne, *Blake*, p. 124 (London, 1906).

These, then, are some of the effects which belong strictly to the subject of prose-rhythm. The next chapter will deal with cadence, which, though bound up with prose-rhythm, may yet be separated from it with advantage for the purpose of analysis.

CHAPTER III

CADENCE

IT is convenient to begin this chapter with an account
of what has been written on the subject of cadence,
before defining and describing cadence itself. Most of
these writings are short essays concerned chiefly with
the classical cadence or *cursus* as it is called. They em-
body data collected by different scholars who, although
working more or less independently of each other, are
not frequently antagonistic, but follow the same direction, some, however, going further than others. Dupli-
cation and overlapping of results is, therefore, common,
and for this reason it is intended, not to give a detailed
account of the work of each individual, but to sum up
the results as a whole.

Although prose-rhythm has long been recognised, and
has been studied by scholars from time to time, the
systematic investigation of cadence is a comparatively
recent development. A French writer, Noël Valois,
seems to have been one of the earliest of modern
inquirers in this field, with his tract on the art of
letter-writing in France in the Middle Ages, which was
published in 1880 and discussed the appearance of the
cursus in this particular form of prose. Further re-
searches by other scholars showed that the use of the
cursus was not confined to letter-writing and opened

out a wide field. The work of Valois and Havet in
France, of Meyer in Germany, and of Zielinski in
Russia, is well known. The studies in English are all
confined to short articles. Professor Clark has written
four, all dealing with the *cursus*: the first, published in
1905 in the *Classical Review* (XIX, pp. 164–72), is a
digest of Zielinski's conclusions; the second, *Fontes
Prosae Numerosae* (1909), is a "sylva" of quotations
from the ancients on prose-rhythm in general with a
preface on the *cursus*; the third and fourth are both
reprints of lectures, *The Cursus in Mediaeval and Vulgar
Latin* (1910) giving a history of the *cursus*, and *Prose-
Rhythm in English* (1913) discussing both classical and
non-classical cadences. In the *Church Quarterly Review*
for April 1912 there is an article by Mr Shelly, *Rhythmical Prose in Latin and English*, on the *cursus* in the
English Prayer-Book with special reference to the
Collects. Professor Elton's *A Sheaf of Papers* (1922)
contains a paper, already mentioned in another connection, "English Prose Numbers", reprinted from
Essays and Studies of the English Association, vol. IV
(1913), which is concerned with prose-rhythm and
cadence. Mr Croll also discusses *cursus* and other
cadences in his paper "The Cadence of English Oratorical
Prose" in *Studies in Philology* (University of North
Carolina, January 1919). With the exception of an
article by the present writer on "Rhythm in the Prose
of Sir Thomas Browne" in the *Review of English
Studies*, July 1927, which contained analysis of rhythm

from the point of view of cadence as well as of prose-rhythm, these seem to be all the available writings in English, other than short notes, on the subject of cadence.

THE *CURSUS*

I. *In Latin*

The ancients considered, as we do, that their sentences were built up of separate parts which they called " commata " and " cola ", whilst the sentence itself they called " period ". They believed that the whole sentence was pervaded by rhythm or " number ", but the ends of the " period ", " cola ", and " commata " were rhythmically the most important parts of the sentence. In these places, particularly at the end of the " period ", they aimed at special rhythmical effect. For this purpose certain definite successions or sequences of feet seem to have been favoured ; these are the *cursus*, so called because the name implies " a run ", thus suiting the trochaic movement which was an essential part of their composition. The *cursus* served the Greeks instead of punctuation and their familiarity with its forms may be judged from the fact that in a monotonous address, Longinus tells us, " knowing beforehand the endings as they become due, people actually beat time with the speakers, and get before them, and render the movement too soon as though in a dance ".[1] " The cursus ", writes

[1] Longinus, *On the Sublime*, Section xli (trans. A. O. Prickard, Oxford, 1906).

Professor Elton, "is a name for certain sequences of feet which come in emphatic places and are used because they are thought to be more beautiful and effective than others".[1] Professor Clark tells us that " whenever the speaker paused to draw fresh breath, he punctuated by a *numerus*, or cadence ".[2]

Thrasymachus of Chalcedon seems to have been the first writer to introduce the *cursus* into his prose deliberately; previous writers had used it by accident. He was followed by Isocrates and Demosthenes, the latter making frequent use of a cretic followed by trochee or spondee, double trochee or double spondee. In the hands of later writers, particularly those connected with Asia, the double trochee became the favourite ending. Professor Clark tells us that "The Romans adopted the use of *numeri* from Asiatic teachers before the Ciceronian era",[3] and we find Cicero attempting to give rules for the *cursus* in his *Orator*. Not only was he a theorist on the subject, but also used the *cursus* in his speeches, and from these much of our information has been obtained.

From an analysis of Cicero's speeches Zielinski discovered that the *cursus* appeared in three main forms, and was able to give the following rule: "In every clausula there are two parts, a basis and a cadence. The basis consists of a cretic or its metrical equivalent,

---

[1] "English Prose Numbers", in *A Sheaf of Papers*, p. 143.

[2] *Prose Rhythm in English*, p. 3.

[3] *The Cursus in Mediaeval and Vulgar Latin*, p. 6 (Oxford, 1910).

the cadence varies in length, and is trochaic in character".[1] The three favourite forms in Cicero are:

1. $- \cup - - \asymp$ e.g. vōcĕ tēstātŭr.
2. $- \circ - - \cup \asymp$ e.g. nōstră cūrātĭō.
3. $- \circ - - \cup - \asymp$ e.g. flūmĭnūm quæ tĕnētĭs.

It will be noticed that the base in 2 and 3 may be either
a cretic or a molossus. Any long syllable could be
replaced by two shorts, a possible variation of Form 1
being first paeon and trochee, "ĕssĕ vĭdĕātŭr", and
the trochaic cadence was sometimes prolonged another
syllable, thus giving us another form (4), "spīrĭtūm
pērtĭnēscĕrēm". The variety of endings used by sub-
sequent writers became limited and reached an extreme
in the highly monotonous prose of Symmachus (350–
420).

We are told, however, that although orator and poets
based their rhythm and metre on quantity, accent
persisted in ordinary speech, and, as the quantitative
writers became increasingly artificial, a rhythmical
prose dependent on accent came into use. This change
was a gradual process, and, from the fourth to the
sixth centuries, Latin writers used rhythm based now
on quantity, now on accent. Professor Clark tells us that,
as a rule, in the clausulae of Cicero "accent" and "ictus"
coincide,[2] but this was not always the case with other
writers.

---

[1] Quoted by Professor Clark in *Classical Review*, xix, p. 166.
[2] *The Cursus in Mediaeval and Vulgar Latin*, p. 10.

The result of the enfeeblement of quantity and the stress of the accent was to produce what some writers have called a *cursus mixtus*, a very convenient term which means that some of the clausulae are metrical, while others follow the accent without regard to the quantity. All that is necessary is to have the accents in the right place. The result is that the metrical prose of Saint Cyprian, Symmachus, and Sidonius gives way to accentual or rhythmical prose. Form 1 is succeeded by a rhythmical equivalent consisting of five syllables, e.g. "génus humánum", Form 2 by one of six, e.g. "bóna remédia", and Form 3 by one of seven, e.g. "fáciunt mèritórum". We also find accentual equivalents for other metrical clausulae, e.g. "víctor reditúrus" = "ĕssĕ vīdĕātŭr" (1²),[1] and "(excell)éntiae véstrae scríbere" = "ōptĭmō iūrĕ cōntĭgĭt" (4).[1]

Thus the three chief forms of the *cursus* changed as follows:

$$1. \; -\cup--\smile \quad \text{became} \quad \acute{\,}\sim\sim\acute{\,}\sim$$
$$2. \; -\triangledown--\cup\smile \quad \text{,,} \quad \acute{\,}\sim\sim\acute{\,}\sim\sim$$
$$3. \; -\triangledown--\cup-\smile \quad \text{,,} \quad \acute{\,}\sim\sim\sim\sim\acute{\,}\sim$$

Meyer tells us that it became the rule that "before the last unaccented syllable in each sentence there must be at least two (generally two or four, more rarely three) unaccented syllables".[2]

The use of the *cursus* declined during the seventh and eighth centuries but was revived again in the eleventh, when it was adopted by the Roman Curia, and Pope Gregory, who became Pope in 1187, published rules

---

[1] *The Cursus in Mediaeval and Vulgar Latin*, pp. 10–11. N.B. the term "metrical" is here used to mean "quantitative" as distinct from "accentual".

[2] A. C. Clark, *Fontes Prosae Numerosae*, p. 7.

for its use. According to Professor Clark, the use of the *cursus* "became universal in Papal Bulls, letters, privileges, dispensations, indulgences, and excommunications. It was used in sermons, prayers, collects, chants, and graces. We also find it in non-ecclesiastical literature".[1] About this time also, names for the three chief forms of the *cursus* came into use. Form 1 was called *planus*, Form 2 *tardus*, Form 3 *velox*. The Latin Collect of the Angelus, quoted by Mr Shelly,[2] contains the three forms:

> Gratiam tuam, quaesumus, Domine, mentibus *nóstris infúnde.*
> (Form 1 *cursus planus.*)
> Ut qui, angelo nuntiante, Christi filii tui incarnatiónem cog-
> nóvimus.   (Form 2 *cursus tardus.*)
> Per passionem eius et crucem ad resurrectionis *glóriam per-
> ducámur.*   (Form 3 *cursus velox.*)

It is now considered that the *cursus velox* carried a secondary accent on the fourth syllable, thus, "glóriam pèrducámur", ′×× ′×′×. This style of writing died out again, in the fourteenth and fifteenth centuries, with the coming of the Renaissance.

II. *In English*

Cadences equivalent to the Latin *cursus* are to be found in English prose. Exactly how or why they came there is matter of doubt, but it seems probable that the

---

[1] *The Cursus in Mediaeval and Vulgar Latin*, p. 17.

[2] "Rhythmical Prose in Latin and English", in *Church Quarterly Review*, April 1912, p. 90.

translators of the Bible and the authors of the Prayer-Book had more than a little to do with it, and it is tolerably certain that the *cursus* made its appearance in English through Latin influence. Some writers consider this influence to be direct; that the translators of the Bible and the Collects consciously endeavoured to imitate the rhythm of the *cursus*. But it seems more probable that the translators were unconsciously influenced by the rhythm of their originals, and, endeavouring to obtain a similar rhythmical movement in their translations, reproduced the *cursus* forms without direct or specific imitation. However this may be, allowing for the fundamental differences between the two languages, cadences equivalent to the Latin *cursus* are a feature of English rhythmical prose.

During its naturalisation into English prose, the *cursus* became modified to suit the monosyllabic and dissyllabic character of the English language. Thus, although the number of syllables and the position of the accents remain unchanged, the English *cursus* frequently contains more words and, consequently, more caesuras than the Latin, and the stressed monosyllable makes its appearance. A single example will make this clear: perhaps the nearest approach to *planus* in English would be a sequence such as "cóuntless misfórtunes" ("vóces testántur"), but common equivalents are "cómely and gráceful" and "jóy of redémption". In the English *velox*, the secondary accent tends to be strengthened, thus giving us not only ′× ×ˌ×′×, but also ′× ×′×′×, the latter form being more frequent than the former. There are also certain sequences, both in Latin and English, which may be considered as extensions of the *cursus* forms.

All forms of the *cursus*, both Latin and English, and of other cadences which do not conform to the *cursus* types, begin with a strong stress. Building upon this, Mr Croll[1] has devised a handy system of notation which is almost indispensable when describing forms of cadence which, unlike *planus, tardus*, and *velox*, have no names. Numbers are used which give the position of the accented syllables *counting from the end*. Thus, the *cursus planus* (′× ×′×) would be 5–2, the accents occurring on the second and fifth syllables counting from the end, *tardus* (′× ×′× ×) would be 6–3, and *velox* (′× ×`×′× or ′× ×′×′×) 7–4–2, or, if it is wished to show whether the accent on 4 is secondary or strong, the figures could be written 7–4̀–2 or 7–4́–2. In order to prevent mistakes it should be explained why the syllables are always counted from the end, though the reason may be obvious. Since all forms of cadence, classical and non-classical, begin with a strong stress, mere numbering of the accented syllables counting from the beginning would not give the length of the sequence. Every description would begin with the figure 1, thus, both *planus*, ′× ×′×, and *tardus*, ′× ×′× ×, would be 1–4. It is evident that a notation of this kind would be useless.

[1] "The Cadence of English Oratorical Prose", in *Studies in Philology* (Univ. of N. Carolina, Jan. 1919).

The forms of the English *cursus* together with their notations are as follows:

1. *Cursus planus:* ´××´×, 5–2, "cóuntless misfórtunes", "wátching and wáiting", "cóme to recéive it", etc.

   Extension: ´×××´×, 6–2, "(re)márkable advénture", " párdon for offénders", etc.

2. *Cursus tardus:* ´××´××, 6–3, "Cána in Gálilee", "vísion of mémory", etc.

   Extension: ´×××´××, 7–3, "sécrets of philósophy", etc.

3. *Cursus velox:* ´××\×´×, 7–4̇–2, "vápour upòn the móuntains", or, more frequently, ´××´×´×, 7–4̇–2, "súitable Chrístmas présents", "(af)féction may céase to wónder", etc.

   Extension: ´×××´×´×, 8–4–2, "bróke into a thóusand píeces", etc.

4. ´××´×´××, 8–5–3,[1] "tíme of these úrns depósited", etc.

Mr Croll[2] adds a further form ("trispondaic") which is *velox* + one or more extra trochees: ´××´×´×´×, 9–6–4–2, "sáilors are bórn to tóil unénding".

According to Mr Croll,[3] the extension (8–4–2) of *velox*, a common English ending, was not recognised in mediaeval Latin. The "trispondaic" ending is not common in English, and is always difficult to recognise on account of its length and the fact that it frequently contains many prose-feet.

Mr Croll considers that the form 7–3 "is one of the commonest, as it is one of the most beautiful, of English

---

[1] This and other forms of *cursus* and non-classical cadence have no names; Mr Croll's notation thus becoming, in these cases, invaluable.

[2] "The Cadence of English Oratorical Prose".   [3] *Ibid.*

endings".[1] It is, however, somewhat hazardous to make
comparisons of this kind. The above list does not claim
to be exhaustive. It contains the chief types of *cursus*;
other endings exist which may be looked upon as
extensions of these types. Thus, the ending 10–5–3 may
be encountered, "cómpliment to his fáther's próbity",
but this shares the disability of all long endings, being
difficult to recognise. The ending 7–5–3 is also to be
found, "áncient mágnanímity".

To sum up, it seems clear that, whatever their origin,
there are certain cadences in English which, allowing
for the differences between the two languages, may be
looked upon as corresponding more or less exactly to
the forms of the Latin *cursus*. There are three chief
forms of English *cursus*, equivalent to the Latin *planus*,
tardus, and *velox*. The *cursus* need not begin with the
beginning of a word, and, within the limits of its form,
may contain any number of words. All forms of the
cursus end on a light syllable.

NATIVE CADENCES

As a general rule, the English language, owing to its
monosyllabic and dissyllabic character, is not easily
adapted to the formation of the *cursus*. Thus, there
are many endings, occurring frequently and possessing
beauty and finish not inferior to the *cursus*, which,
however, bear no resemblance to the *cursus*. The

[1] "The Cadence of English Oratorical Prose", p. 17.

cadences of these endings may be called "native" and, as Professor Elton remarks, "no one has yet gone far with the classification of native cadences or has shown whether or not it is possible to make one".[1] This possibility does, indeed, seem very doubtful for reasons which will appear, but it would be unwise to assert that the task could not be accomplished.

The chief differences between the native cadences and the *cursus* is that the majority of the former end with a strong stress (e.g. "brútish and shórt"), whereas the latter never do so. Mr Shelly[2] notices that this is characteristic of most of those endings in the Sunday and Holy-Day Collects of the Prayer-Book of 1549, which are different from the *cursus*. He gives examples, such as "ármour of líght" and "(con)témpt of thy wórd". Mr Harkness, in a brief note on Sidney and the *cursus*, notices that, in the particular paragraph which he is examining, many of the cadences (eight out of fifteen) are stressed on the final syllable, a phenomenon foreign to Latin. "This deviation from the classical accentual system emphasises specifically the strongly monosyllabic nature of the English vocabulary: 7 of these 8 endings are monosyllables".[3] Professor Saintsbury notices that the use of a monosyllable to end a sentence or paragraph is frequent in English prose, but

[1] "English Prose Numbers", in *Essays and Studies of the English Association*, iv, p. 45.

[2] "Rhythmical Prose in Latin and English", p. 93.

[3] S. Harkness, "The Prose Style of Sir Philip Sidney", in *Univ. of Wisconsin Studies in Language and Literature*, ii, p. 75, 1918.

does not connect this with the cadence. Here, then, is one type, perhaps the most frequent, of native cadence.

1. Beginning and ending with a strong stress and containing only two strong stresses. The number of light syllables between the two strong stresses may vary from one to four, thus making six syllables in the longest form. More than four light syllables may be possible but are rarely found. Thus there are several variations of this one type:

(a) ′×′, 3–1, "wéary bácks", etc. Mr Shelly, asserting that Meyer's law (see p. 77) holds good for native cadences as well as for the *cursus*, condemns this ending as repugnant to English. "The verse endings indeed, such as fórty dáys and fórty níghts, do not comply with this rule ; but a verse ending of a sentence is a fault, as contrary to the spirit of English prose as it is to the metrical prose of Cicero and to the rhythmical prose of the mediaeval *cursus*".[1] To condemn this ending as "contrary to the spirit of English prose" is somewhat sweeping. As a cadence, it is too short to be satisfactory, and, on account of its brevity, it is not sufficiently well-marked to stand easily by itself. Thus it is often found as part of a longer ending in types 2 or 3 *a*, below.

(b) ′××′, 4–1, "chóral lamént", "shíps from the séa", "(at)tíred in her róbes", etc.

(c) ′×××′, 5–1, "lánding on the rócks", "(re)sóunded with the crý", etc. This, and the preceding 4–1 ending, are the most common native cadences.

(d) ′××××′, 6–1, "mótionless as the snów", "(pe)títioning for his són", etc. Owing to the rarity of such successions of light syllables, endings such as this are not very common. Even in this type secondary accent begins to intrude, and if the cadence lengthens out further this intrusion becomes still more prominent.

"Rhythmical Prose in Latin and English", p. 94.

Professor Elton allows a case where no light syllables occur between the accents as, for example, "pále hánds", a spondaic ending. If this is a cadence, it is a very doubtful one ; a mixture of both strong and weak syllables seems necessary to the formation of either native cadence or *cursus*.

2. Cadences of the type ′×′×′, 5–3–1, "cóld and sílent mán". Similar endings are ′× ×′×′, 6–3–1, "(e)mítting a pláintive nóte", and ′× × ×′×′, 7–3–1, "(un)knówn among the Híghland hílls". Any extension further than this is uncommon, and secondary accent tends to appear. Owing to the completeness of the 4–1 and 5–1 cadences, the presence of more than one light syllable between the last two accents of the 5–3–1 type tends to break up the long cadence by forming a 4–1 or 5–1 ending.

3. Cadences containing clash of strong stresses foreign to *cursus* forms. These may be divided into two main types:

(*a*) Those ending on a strong stress, as for example ′×″, 4–2–1, "míle or twó hígh", or ′× ×″, 5–2–1, "nów for the fírst tíme", or ′× × ×″, 6–2–1, "cólouring of púre líght". A different form is ″×′, 4–3–1, "whírlpóol of míst", but extensions beyond this (e.g. 5–4–1) are doubtful for the reason given above in another connection (see type 2).

(*b*) Those ending with a light syllable. Probably the most common are ′×″×, 5–3–2, "kíng of áll Éngland", and ′× ×″×, 6–3–2, "bénding my éye fórward". The ending ″′×, 4–3–2, "dárk réd róses", is less common, and extensions beyond 6–3–2 are rare. As in (*a*) clash of strong stress may occur at the beginning on the type ″×′×, 5–4–2, "scárecrów of Fánny". Any extension further than this is doubtful, owing to the formation of the *planus*, 5–2.

The occurrence of more than three strong stresses in succession in any ending is rare, and an ending so formed is not markedly cadenced.

4. Some native cadences end on a light syllable and have no clash of strong stress. These can only be recognised as native by the fact that, although ending on a light syllable, they do not approximate to any form of the *cursus* or its extensions. An example of such a cadence is "thén the cáre is óver", ′×′×′×, 6–4–2.

The above list of native cadences does not claim to be exhaustive. It is clear that, whilst the forms of the *cursus* are comparatively limited, the varieties of native cadence are many, and, at the present stage of research, impossible to enumerate completely. Mr Croll attempts to formulate rules for cadence[1], but with unsatisfactory results. His first rule states that the English cadence ordinarily begins on one of the syllables 5 to 10, counting from the end; it never begins later than the fifth but sometimes the long cadence may begin as far back as the eleventh syllable, as in 11–7–3, or even the twelfth, 12–8–4, but these are extreme cases.[2] If by English cadence Mr Croll means native cadence as distinct from *cursus,* it is obvious that part, at least, of this rule is untrue. Although it seems that short metrical cadences such as ′×′×, 4–2, "mány wómen", are less emphatic than others, they do exist, and, moreover, one of the commonest and most effective of native cadences begins later than the fifth syllable, ′×·×′, 4–1, "húndreds of mén". A rule that would exclude this from English cadences cannot be defended. Again, long cadences such as those named by Mr Croll are difficult to

[1] M. W. Croll, "The Cadence of English Oratorical Prose", pp. 45–7.
[2] *Ibid.* p. 45.

recognise. The 12–8–4 ending is merely a succession of three first paeons, ′× × ×′× × ×′× × ×, and rare in English. In the other ending, 11–7–3, the *tardus*, 7–3, would probably be immediately recognised and heard to the exclusion of the longer cadence.

Although rules such as these may be misleading, it is possible to enumerate certain features common to all known cadences, but these do not represent rules in the sense that all departures from them will be wrong.

1. All forms of cadence[1] begin with a strongly stressed syllable.

2. Cadences need not begin at the beginning of either foot or word.

3. The most emphatic cadences are those coming at the end of a sentence. Less emphatic are those coming before a colon, semi-colon, or comma.

4. Both strong and weak syllables are necessary to the formation of any cadence.

5. All forms of the *cursus* end on a weak syllable; native cadences may end on either weak or strong.

It is now necessary to connect the first two of these five characteristics with certain remarks which have already been made. In chap. II it was shown that, since there is no difference in sound between logical and rhythmical accents, and, in prose, which does not allow

[1] Cadence is a general term including all forms, whether "native" or *cursus*.

a rhythmical pattern, no difference in position either, the logical and rhythmical groupings coincide. Thus, in scanning the prose-rhythm of a passage, words are never cut by the foot-divisions. The feet, however, may begin with any syllable, strong or weak, and *rising* and *waved* rhythms are more common than *falling* or *level* rhythms. All cadences begin on a strongly stressed syllable and need not begin with the beginning of either word or foot. It is clear, therefore, that cadence and prose-rhythm will seldom coincide. Yet the mind can experience both cadence and prose-rhythm together, and, as Professor Elton says, "this crossing of cadence and prose-rhythm constitutes a beauty when each effect is itself agreeable".[1] Thus, although the prose-feet of the following phrase are:

and with wrécks | of forgótten | delírium,[2]

the final cadence is a *cursus tardus* begining in the middle of a foot:

-gótten delírium.

The method of marking cadences to be followed in the analysis in this book needs some explanation. Vertical lines have already been used for marking foot-divisions, and, since crossed brackets and underlining are impossible to print in the ordinary way, different types are the most suitable means available. All forms of the

---

[1] "English Prose Numbers", in *A Sheaf of Papers*, p. 153.
[2] De Quincey, *Suspiria de Profundis* (*Works*, ed. D. Masson, XIII, p. 366, London, 1897).

cursus are printed in italics, whilst native cadences are in heavy type. Thus, when scanned for both cadence and prose-rhythm, the phrase just quoted will appear as follows:

and with wrécks | of forgótten | *delírium.*

A wider field in the investigation of cadence is opened by Mr Croll's important statement that "the careful student of prose which has a markedly cadenced sound must be aware that this sound cannot be explained as due to the widely separated endings studied, for instance, by Shelly in the Collects. It must be due to cadences that occur with sufficient frequency to produce a pervasive and characteristic effect".[1] In English prose, cadences are not confined to the ends of clauses or sentences but may occur at emphatic places within the sentence. Thus, any phrase which is felt to have unitary character may be cadenced. "The end of any phrase felt as having a unitary character may be cadenced, whether or not it coincides with one of the divisions of period".[2] The following is an example:

…it is like the stare of an *impudent mán of fáshion* at a fine woman, when she first comes into a room.[3]

Here, the unitary phrase "ímpudent man of fashion" is a *cursus velox*, 7–4–2. Although the term *cursus* applied to the ends of "periods", "cola", and "commata" only,

[1] "The Cadence of English Oratorical Prose", p. 40.

[2] *Ibid.* p. 33.

[3] Charles Lamb, *Hospita on Immoderate Indulgence* (*Works*, ed. E. V. Lucas, *Miscellaneous Prose*, p. 145, London, 1912).

it has been found convenient here to use it for all equivalents of classical cadences, no matter where they may occur. It must be recognised that this use, like that of classical names for English feet, is purely a matter of convenience, and the student should remember that, in classical prose-rhythm, the term *cursus* was used to describe the rhythms of the endings of "period", "cola", and "commata".

Cadences occur not only within the sentence, they also frequently overlap. This overlapping is a corollary of the cadencing of unitary phrases within the sentence. It is very common, as Mr Croll points out, when two words, which are often synonymous, are used connected by "and", instead of a single word, and perhaps explains the liking for this practice shown by certain writers. This device is particularly noticeable in rhetorical prose. The overlapping or interlaced cadences may be native or *cursus*, or a mixture of the two. In the following phrase two different types of cadence overlap:

freedom from sórrow and grief.

"Fréedom from sórrow", ′× ×′×, is a *cursus planus*, "sórrow and grief", ′× ×′, is a 4–1 native cadence.

This feature demands further symbols in analysis. It is plain that, when two cadences overlap, there must be some means of showing where one ends and the other begins. Something must be done, therefore, to define the overlapping portion. When the overlapping cadences are different, that is native and *cursus*, the syllables common to both are printed in heavy italic type. Thus, the phrase quoted above will appear:

*freedom from **sorrow** and* **grief,**

or, if scanned for prose-rhythm also:

fréedom | from sórrow | and **grief,**

When the cadences are not mixed, but overlap in the same types, that is native crossing native, and *cursus* crossing *cursus*, the only way of indicating the limits of each cadence is by giving them separately in footnotes, a tedious but apparently unavoidable process. The following is an instance of interlaced *cursus*:

múddy and immédiate ínterests.

The whole of this phrase will appear in italics and a footnote will give the length of each *cursus*: "múddy and immédiate", *tardus*, 7–3, "-médiate ínterests", *tardus*, 6–3.

A similar process will be used when native cadences overlap:

lást trémbling cólours of púre líght.

This phrase will be printed in heavy roman type, and the cadences given in a footnote: "lást trémbling cólours", 5–4–2, and "cólours of púre líght", 5–2–1.

It should now be possible to consider the incidence of cadence in order to point out some of its uses and effects.

Perhaps the most obvious and important effects are those which may be obtained by balance and variation of endings, thus giving a "law and order" to the rhythm and supplying a great part of the necessary element of recurrence.

Correspondence of sentence-ends frequently plays a large part in the construction of a rhythmical paragraph, as the following example will show:

First, it may be said that the prophecies have not been, and never will be, fulfilled in the letter, because they contain expressions and statements which do not admit, or certainly have not, a líteral méaning. Thus, in one of the passages just now quoted, it is said that David shall féed the chósen péople. Now, by David, cannot be meant anyone but Christ; that is, the prophecy is figurative; for if one part is not literal, whý should anóther be? Again, it is said that "the Sun of Righteousness shall arise with healing in His wings"; and "behold I will bring forth My Servant the Branch"; and again, "The wolf shall dwell with the lamb, and the leopard shall lie down with the kid". Again, "I will write My law in their hearts". The fulfilment of the prophecy then is either spiritual, or, when it admits of being taken líterally, it is fúture.[1]

Here, with the exception of the quotations, all the sentences end on a light syllable:

$$5\text{--}2,\ 6\text{--}4\text{--}2,\ 6\text{--}3,\ \text{and}\ 8\text{--}2,$$

and it is noticeable that the only one which is accented further from the end than the second syllable is an interrogative ending, which, by lengthening out in this way, seems to leave the question hanging in the air. All

---

[1] J. H. Newman, *Sermons on Subjects of the Day*, No. 14, p. 209 (London, 1844).

cadences, whether native or *cursus,* ending on a light syllable have a similarity of effect; in the same way, cadences ending on a strong syllable correspond.

Sentences frequently show correspondence of "commata" and "cola" endings, as, for example, the following:

There was more between them now thán there had éver been, but it had céased to sèparáte them, it sustained them in fact like a deep water on whích they flóated clóser.[1]

The scansion of "than there had ever been" is doubtful. There is little doubt that the first syllable of "ever" is accented and there is a strong tendency for an accent to be set up on "than", thus completing the *tardus.* This tendency to set up an accent on a syllable which is not definitely accented, or to strengthen an existing secondary accent in order to complete a cadence, and particularly a *cursus,* is frequently noticeable. The other parts of the sentence end 6–4̇–2 and 6–4́–2 respectively, the movement thus being very closely correspondent.

Correspondence of strong endings, that is those in which the last syllable is accented, is shown in this paragraph:

I watched the greying of the dawn suspíring into róse. Then a yellow ripple came out of the narrow corrie at the súmmit of the híll. The yellow ripple ran like the running tide through the flushing grey, and washed in among the sprays of a birch beside me and among the rowan-clústers of a móuntain-ásh. But at the falling of the sun the yellow ripple was an ebbing tide, and the sprays of the birch were as a perishing flame and the

[1] Henry James, "The Papers", in *The Better Sort,* p. 311 (London, 1903).

rowan-berries were réd as dróps of blóod. Thereafter I watched the rose slow fading into the gréy véils of dúsk. O greying of my dawn suspiring into rose: O grey veils of dusk that obscure the tender flushings of my róse-lít dáwn![1]

All the sentences in this paragraph end on a strongly stressed syllable and the cadences are respectively

5–1, 5–1, 7–3–1, 5–3–1, 4–3–1, and 3–2–1.

The last ending (3–2–1) is too heavy to be a true cadence and contains only one type of stress, whereas both strong and weak stresses are necessary to the formation of cadence (see p. 87). It may, however, be argued that this ending is cadenced 7–3–2–1, "flúshings of my róse-lít dáwn", but this is doubtful because the molossus ending seems to be too heavy to combine easily with other syllables to form a cadence. The gradual closing up of, and elimination of weak syllables in, the cadences at the ends of the successive sentences is a noteworthy feature, especially since gradation is seldom so precise:

7–3–1, 5–3–1, 4–3–1, 3–2–1.

The effect is to give added emphasis to the molossus, itself a rare foot in English prose, which closes the paragraph.

A similar correspondence of minor endings is shown in the following sentence:

The wasting away of the flesh is less appárent in the fáce; and one might imagine that in this sweet marble countenance was

[1] Fiona Macleod, in *Anthology of Imaginative Prose*, pp. 315–16 (ed. R. P. Cowl).

seen the very sáme upon whích, eléven yéars agó, her mother's darkened eyes had língered to the lást, until clouds had swallowed up the vísion of her belóved twíns.[1]

The endings here are cadenced 5–1, 4–1, 5–3–1, 5–1, and 8–3–1 (taking "belóved" as a trisyllable). Distinct prominence is thus given to the 4–1 and 5–1 type of cadence.

The construction, however, of rhythmical paragraphs by means of a series of cadences all of which end on the same kind of syllable, strong or weak as the case may be, is not the method most frequently employed. Paragraph rhythm, and sentence rhythm too, is more frequently built up of both strong and weak endings, carefully alternated and balanced.

The following is an illustration:

The presence that thus rose so strangely beside the waters, is expressive of what in the ways of a thousand years man had cóme to desíre. Hers is the head upon which all "the ends of the world are come", and the eyelids are a líttle wéary. It is a beauty wrought out from within upon the flesh, the deposit, little cell by cell, of strange thoughts and fantastic reveries and exquísite pássions. Set it for a moment beside one of those white Greek goddesses or beautiful women of antiquity, and how would they be troubled by this beauty, into which the soul with all its máladies has pássed? All the thoughts and experience of the world have etched and moulded there, in that which they have of power to refine and make expressive the outward form, the animalism of Greece, the lust of Rome, the reverie of the middle age with

[1] De Quincey, *Suspiria de Profundis* (*Works*, ed. D. Masson, XIII, pp. 356–7, London, 1897).

its spiritual ambition and imaginative love, the return of the
Pagan world, the síns of the Bórgias. She is older than the rocks
among which she sits; like the vampire, she has been dead many
times, and learned the secrets of the grave; and has been a diver
in deep seas, and keeps their fallen day about her; and trafficked
for strange webs with Eastern merchants; and, as Leda, was the
mother of Helen of Troy, and, as Saint Anne, the mother of
Mary; and all this has been to her but as the sound of lyres and
flutes, and lives only in the delicacy with which it has moulded
the changing lineaments, and tinged the éyelìds and the hánds.
The fancy of a perpetual life, sweeping together ten thousand
experiences, is an old one; and modern thought has conceived
the idea of humanity as wrought upon by, and summing up in
itself, áll módes of thóught and lífe. Certainly Lady Lisa might
stand as the embodiment of the old fancy, the symbol of the
módern idéa.[1]

The endings in this paragraph show careful adjustment and correspond as follows:

Sentence A,	cóme to desíre,	′××′,	4-1.
B,	líttle wéary,	′×′×,	4-2.
C,	-quísite pássions,	′×′×,	4-2.
D,	máladies has pássed,	′×××′,	5-1.
E,	síns of the Bórgias,	′××′××,	6-3.
F,	éyelìds and the hánds,	∩××′,	5-4-1.
G,	módes of thóught and lífe,	′×′×′,	5-3-1.
H,	módern idéa,	′××′×,	5-2.

The double trochee cadence of ending B accords
admirably with the sense of weariness conveyed by the
words. Correspondence throughout is marked, but is
never so identical as to suggest metre.

[1] Walter Pater, *La Gioconda.*

Correspondence of both strong and weak "commata" and "cola" endings is to be found in the following sentence:

In this work, when it shall be found that múch is omítted, let it not be forgotten that much líkewíse is perfórmed; and though no book is ever spared out of ténderness to the áuthor, and the world is little solicitous to know whence proceeded the faults of thát which it condémns, yet it may gratify curiosity to inform it that the English Dictionary was written with little assístance of the léarned, and without any pátronage of the gréat; not in the soft obscurities of retirement or under the shelter of ácadémic bówers, but amidst inconvénience and distráction, in síckness and in sórrow.[1]

The endings of this sentence correspond closely, as the following table will show:

múch is omítted,	′× ×′×,	5–2.
líkewíse is perfórmed,	″× ×′,	5–4–1.
ténderness to the áuthor,	′× × × ×′×,	7–2.
thát which it condémns,	′× × ×′,	5–1.
-sístance of the léarned,	′× × ×′×,	6–2.
pátronage of the gréat,	′× × × ×′,	6–1.
ácadémic bówers,	′×′×′×,	6–4–2 ("bowers" is doubtful; it may be a monosyllable).
-vénience and distráction,	′× × ×′×,	6–2
(or, if "-venience" be taken as a trisyllable,	′× ×, 7–2).	
síckness and in sórrow,	′× × ×′×,	6–2.

It will be noticed that cadences such as 6–4–2 or 5–3–1 ("academic bowers") seem to be continuous rather than final, and do not form emphatic endings.

[1] Johnson, *Preface to the Dictionary*.

In correspondence of cadence, as in sequences of prose-feet, repetition is to be avoided; a succession of endings which are all cadenced in the same way is monotonous and unsuited to good prose.

Interweaving of cadence is prominent in most prose of a highly "numerous" character, of which the following is an example:

...and **hów** | **through the cúrdling** | **wréaths** | of the réstless | **cráshing** | **abýss** | **belów,** | the *blúe* | *of the wáter,* | **páled** | **by the** *fóam* | *in its bódy,* | shòws : **púrer** | **than the ský** | through whíte ráin-clóud, | while the *shúddering* | *íris* | stóops | in *trémulous* | **stíllness** | **over áll,** | *fáding* | *and flúshing* | *altér-nately*[1] | through the chóking | **spráy** | **and sháttered** | **sún-shine. ...**[2]

The percentage of *cursus* endings is here particularly great, but the major endings more frequently close with a strong than with a weak stress. Two groups:

hów through the cúrdling wréaths, ′× ×′×′,

and

cráshing abýss belów, ′× ×′×′,

are closely correspondent. "Crashing" is a very suitable epithet, its trochaic rhythm disturbing the flow of the sentence and thereby affording a rhythmical suggestion of the tumult of the falls. The almost metrical undulation of

fáding and flushing alternately

---

[1] Here two *cursus* overlap:

"fáding and flúshing", 5–2, planus.
"flúshing altérnately", 6–3, tardus.

[2] Cowl, *Anthology of Imaginative Prose*, p. 273.

is marked, and is another instance of the apt accordance
of rhythm with sense. Metrical movement, however, is
not induced, because the suggestion of metre does not
persist but is broken by the change in movement which
follows.

At the present stage of research little more can be
said about the principal effects or uses of cadence. The
most important of these is sentence and paragraph formation by correspondence of endings, a correspondence
which, in paragraphs, binds the rhythmical threads
into a continuous chain. In the smaller units of sentence
and phrase, interwoven cadences are often prominent,
and it may prove useful to study to what extent these
subdue the prose-rhythm. There are, however, certain
minor devices which must be noticed before concluding.

Correspondence of rhythm and sense is an essential
feature of the best "numerous" prose. Rhythm and
syntax should coincide, and for this reason it seems
that, although cadences are frequently so common as to
pervade sentences and paragraphs, there is one place at
which cadence should not occur. This is at a point
immediately before the end of a syntactical group,
especially if that group be the end of a sentence. The
following example will explain what is meant:

...so much are we immersed in our *múddy* | *and immédiate* |
interests | that we think, | ....[1]

[1] Hilaire Belloc, *The Path to Rome*, p. 179 (London, 1923).
Here two *cursus* overlap:

"múddy and immédiate", 7–3, extension of *tardus.*
"-médiate interests", 6–3, *tardus.*

This cadencing of "a non-final unitary phrase", as it is termed by Mr Croll, causes the words which follow the cadence (in this case "that we think") to be a mere appendix spoiling its finality.

Similarly, when a sentence is fully cadenced at the beginning, the pitch should be maintained throughout or the rhythm will suffer not a little. The following sentence begins with many beautiful cadences, but the end does not fulfil its promise:

Its *ténder* | *simplícity,* | its translúcent | dépth | of páthos, | its *swéetness* | *and its trúthfulness,* | may be félt | on a fírst | réading; | but its *márvellous* | *quálity* | *of èxecútion,*[1] | the súbtle | mágic | of its stýle, | the incómparable | and instínctive | chóice | of phráse | which màkes : a míracle | of évery | líne, | can only and can hardly be appreciated in full after longer and more loving study, than any but the masterpieces of lyric poetry deserve and require and reward.[2]

The unhurried sweetness of music of the first part of the sentence (to "reading") becomes slightly quicker and harsher in the words which follow (to "every line"), and the ending is disappointing. There is a noticeable tendency to stress the syllable "ex" in "quálity of èxecútion" in order to complete the *cursus velox*. The tendency for a stress to be set up on a weakly stressed

---

[1] Here two *cursus* overlap:

      "márvellous quálity", 6–3, *tardus.*

      "quálity of èxecútion", 8–4–2, extension of *velox.*

[2] Swinburne, *Studies in Prose and Poetry (Toute la lyre),* p. 272 (London, 1897).

syllable, or for a secondary stress to be strengthened, in order to complete a cadence, is a common feature in "numerous" prose. The following sentence contains an example of the strengthening of secondary stress:

The day begins again; and how wonderful is the return of the day, híll after híll | rísing ŏ́ut | of the shádow.[1]

The secondary stress on "out" is here considerably strengthened by the suggestion of *cursus planus*, "out of the shadow".

Owing to its binding effect, cadence may be used to lessen the break caused by a pause. This frequently occurs in enumerations where words logically belonging together are separated by commas, as in this example:

Chárity | súffereth | lóng, | and is kínd.[2]

The tendency to form a final 4–1 cadence here links the words "and is kind" to the rhythm of the remainder of the sentence, to which they are already linked by sense. The movement may, at first sight, appear to be almost metrical:

Charity suffereth long, and is kind (ˊ× ×ˊ× ×ˊ× ×ˊ),

but the prose-feet are insistent, and, aided by the pause, cut across the metrical feet and keep the movement within the bounds of prose:

ˊ× × | ˊ× × | ˊ, || × ×ˊ.

[1] George Moore, *The Brook Kerith*, p. 291 (London, 1927).
[2] *Authorised Version of the Bible*, 1 Cor., chap. xiii.

Finally, one more adjustment which should be noticed is contained in the following sentence:

O éloquent, | júst | and míghty | Déath! | whom nóne | could advíse, | *thóu* | *hast persuáded*; | what nóne | hath dáred, | thóu | hast dóne; | and whòm : áll : the wórld | hath fláttered, | thóu ónly | hast cást óut | of the wórld | and despíced; | thóu | hast dráwn | togéther | all the fár-strétched | gréatness, | all the príde, | crúelty, | and ambítion | of mán, | and cóvered it | áll óver | with these twó | nárrow | wórds, | Híc | jácet![1]

The first five major endings here are contracted in accordance with the increasing emphasis, and are cadenced 5–3–1, 4–1, 5–2, 3–1, 3–1, thus giving an air of finality to the assertion "what none hath dared, thou hast done". The next ending lengthens out to 6–4–2 ("áll the wórld hath fláttered"), thus forming an effective "middle" to the sentence-rhythm. This sentence is a striking example of the beauty and effectiveness of native cadences which are present almost to the exclusion of the *cursus*.

A further instance of the contraction of endings for emphasis is present in this sentence from Browne:

There is a nearer way to Heaven than Homer's chain; an easy logick may conjoin a heaven and éarth in one árgument, and with léss than a sorítes, resolve áll thíngs to Gód.[2]

---

[1] Raleigh, *History of the World* (*Selections*, ed. G. E. Hadow, p. 117, Oxford, 1917).

The overlapping cadences in this passage are: "óut of the wórld", 4–1, and "wórld and despíced", 4–1.

[2] Sir T. Browne, *Religio Medici*, I, xviii, 51–4.

Here again the finality of the contracted and strongly stressed ending, "áll thíngs to Gód", accords admirably with the sense.

Cadence has now been defined and explained and comments have been made upon its chief uses and effects and on some of its minor adjustments. For the present purpose it is unnecessary to proceed further; the student should now be able to recognise and notice for himself the principal features of both prose-rhythm and cadence in the work of any author. The coalition of prose-rhythm and cadence results in "numerous" prose, whose rhythm can be as beautiful and satisfying to the ear as that of the best poetry.

CHAPTER IV

SOME APPLICATIONS

IT has been shown that the rhythm of English prose
possesses two important elements, prose-rhythm and
cadence. The first of these consists of syllables grouped
together according to the sense into "feet", whose
stresses are logical as opposed to metrical in verse. The
rhythm set up in the mind by these groups in prose has
been termed in this book "prose-rhythm"; in the scansion of this foot-divisions never cut the words. There
are many features such as gradation of feet, phrases,
clauses, or sentences, which belong to prose-rhythm and
which were discussed in chap. II. There are also many
others which have not been noticed in this book; in
addition to those which are already known there
are probably others awaiting discovery. Prose-rhythm
exists in most prose. Even ordinary conversation may
be rhythmical, but it is found that in the lowest forms
of prose, scansion and division by feet are extremely
difficult and sometimes impossible, whereas "numerous"
prose tends to scan itself.

It is also found that cadence is rarely, if ever, present
in any marked degree in prose which has no claims to
be rhythmical, whereas it is an important ingredient in
"numerous" prose and is frequently pervasive. Cadence,
we saw, is the name for certain rhythmical sequences
which occur in emphatic places and are apparently

used, either consciously or unconsciously, by writers because they appear to be more effective than others. In highly "numerous" prose cadences occur with great frequency and sometimes overlap. Cadences, it was shown, are of two kinds; those which may be regarded as equivalent to the classical *cursus* and their extensions and which may be conveniently grouped under the name *cursus*, and those which do not conform to any type of the *cursus* and may therefore be called *native*. It is a fact of much importance that some cadences end on a weak, others on a strong, stress, and it is by the skilful alternation, variation, and adjustment of these that many writers build up the rhythm of their sentences and paragraphs. Cadence need not begin with the beginning or end with the end of a word, and, therefore, frequently cuts across the prose-rhythm. This crossing of cadence and prose-rhythm can be, and frequently is, very effective. Cadence must not be confused with those snatches of metre, usually blank verse, which sometimes occur in prose; the forms of cadence are not metrical forms.

PROSE AND VERSE

This brings us to the fascinating, and controversial, subject of the relationship between prose-rhythm and metre. A few scattered observations on this matter will not be out of place here, though the student should remember that the relationship is so indefinite as to be impatient of rigid definition. There are, however, certain essential differences between prose and verse which are almost generally recognised. Perhaps the most important of these, already stated, is that in metre there is a pattern or norm which persists throughout and to which all modulations are referred by the mind, whereas, in prose, there is no such pattern. When expectancy begins to be induced, a metrical element appears. Secondly, on account of this pattern, in metre, the predominant accents are metrical, and feet may be composed of parts of words, but in prose the grouping is logical and feet are made up of whole words.

All this seems quite simple, and there is, of course, no difficulty in distinguishing between, say, the poems of Tennyson and the prose of Newman. However, some of the later blank verse of Shakespeare, and of the Restoration dramatists, with its large percentage of run-on lines, offers a more difficult problem. The following passage is taken from *The Winter's Tale*:

> I say she's dead, I'll swear't. If word nor oath
> Prevail not, go and see: if you can bring
> Tincture or lustre in her lip, her eye,
> Heat outwardly or breath within, I'll serve you
> As I would do the gods.[1]

A passage from Massinger's *Virgin-Martyr* may also be considered:

> No, but pitying,
> For my part, I, that you lose ten times more
> By torturing me, than I that dare your tortures:

[1] *The Winter's Tale*, iii, ii, ll. 203-7.

Through all the army of my sins, I have even
Laboured to break, and cope with death to the face.
The visage of a hangman frights not me;
The sight of whips, racks, gibbets, axes, fires,
Are scaffoldings by which my soul climbs up
To an eternal habitation.[1]

Let us suppose that these two passages had been written as follows:

I sáy she's déad, I'll swéar't. If wórd nor óath prevàil not, gó and sée: if yŏu can bríng tíncture or lústre in her líp, her éye, héat óutwardly or bréath withín, I'll sérve yóu as I wóuld do the góds;

and

Nó, but pítying, for mý párt, I, that you lóse tén tímes móre by tórturing me, than Í that dáre your tórtures: through áll the ármy òf my síns, I have éven láboured to bréak, and cópe with déath to the fáce. The vísage of a hángman fríghts not mé; the síght of whíps, rácks, gíbbets, áxes, fíres, are scáffoldings by whích my sóul climbs úp to an etérnal hăbitátion.

At first sight both extracts may now appear to be in prose, but the former at least is easily recognised as belonging to poetry. The succession of iambic feet is so pronounced as to become established as a base which persists in the mind throughout all modulations from it. The lines from Massinger present more difficulty but the iambic movement again asserts itself and metrical stress occurs, as, for instance, on "of" in "áll

---

[1] *The Virgin-Martyr*, II, iii (Mermaid ed., II, pp. 320–1).

the ármy òf my síns". Moreover, in both passages the diction and syntax, especially the latter, arouse suspicion that they do not belong to prose. Such arrangements as "If word nor oath prevail not" and "The visage of a hangman frights not me" are not common in prose, but are so frequent in verse as to be almost characteristic. Passages such as these are "verse invaded by prose emphasis";[1] they remain metrical and can be recognised as such, even when written without line-division.

Approaching the borders of prose and poetry we come to free-verse and stave prose-poetry such as Macpherson's *Ossian*. The following are two examples of free-verse:

Lúmbermen in their wínter cámp, dáy-bréak in the
   wóods, strípes of snów on the límbs of trées, the occásional
                                 snápping,
The glád clèar sóund of one's vóice, the mérry sóng, the
   nátural lífe of the wóods, the stróng dáy's wórk,
The blázing fíre at níght, the swéet táste of súpper, the
   tálk; the béd of hémlock bóughs, and the béar-skín.[2]

The Vícar, I belíeve, would líke to óffer públic práyer
   for the retúrn of the wánderer.
And the Dóctor, I knów, is a líttle unhínged and
   cúring péople out of púre ábsence of mínd.
For mý párt I have hópe; and the tróusers I dis-
   cárded last wéek will nót be gíven awáy just yét.[3]

---

[1] D. S. MacColl, "Rhythm in English Verse, Prose and Speech" (*Essays and Studies of the English Association*, v, p. 50).

[2] Walt Whitman, *The Lumbermen's Camp (Song of the Broad-Axe)*.

[3] E. V. Lucas, *Jack*, verse 11.

Although the length of the lines in these two passages remains fairly regular, such is by no means the case in much free-verse and any attempt to test according to the number of syllables in the line is almost certain to be unsuccessful. The question thus arises why the lines are given any particular length and why the poem should not be written as prose. The lines from Lucas seem little different from prose. They are, it is true, end-stopped, and the first stop at least would not be required, and would probably be omitted, in prose. The language is not above the level of ordinary prose. If, however, we read the passage aloud, laying special emphasis on the accented syllables, it will be noticed that the intervals between them are so regular as to set up a definite lilt which is expected to continue, and does so, throughout. This lilt, although not necessarily strong enough to cause the constant formation of verse-feet, is yet definite enough to prevent prose-grouping from predominating, and, indeed, metrical sequences do occur, and occur frequently, thus strengthening the lilt. The following are examples:

would líke | to óf|fer púb|lic práyer;
and the Dóc|tor, I knów, | is a lít|tle unhínged;
I have hópe; | and the tróu|sers I discár|ded last wéek.

It is noticeable that these sequences all contain the same number of feet and that the rhythm changes at the end of each line. The repetition thus established is too regular to be a prose effect.

The lines from Whitman are an instance of that

enumeration, almost a kind of catalogue, which is a feature of much free-verse and is in itself an effect alien to true prose. From the point of view of syntax this poem is incomplete, being merely a collection of nouns and adjectives, joined by conjunctions, and not possessing a single verb. This fact alone would rouse suspicion even if the lines were written as a prose paragraph. Moreover, there is an obvious regularity of beat, especially in the second and third lines, which should not be present in good prose. The number of syllables separating the accents varies very little; for the most part it is either one or two.

The difference between stave prose-poetry and prose is usually marked, as in this paragraph, taken at random from Macpherson's *Ossian*:

Night is dull and dark. The clouds rest on the hills. No star with green trembling beam, no moon, looks from the sky. I hear the blast in the woods; but I hear it distant far. The stream of the valley murmurs; but its murmur is sullen and sad. From the tree at the grave of the dead the long-howling owl is heard. I see a dim form on the plain! It is a ghost! It fades, it flies. Some funeral shall pass this way; the meteor marks the path.[1]

In this passage, again, there is a regularity of beat, inducing a lilt which persists, and is expected to persist, throughout. Other features, such as the quality of the diction, emphasise the poetic character of such writing, but, from the present point of view, the lilt is the most important.

[1] *Anthology of Imaginative Prose* (ed. R. P. Cowl).

Thus, in all the extracts which we have examined there is a persistent lilt which prevents definite prose-grouping. Although the form of both free-verse and stave prose-poetry is much more elastic than that of normal verse, the quality which arouses expectancy is present in varying degrees. This is a touchstone by which verse and prose may be distinguished. In the hybrid forms which we have been considering there is expectancy which definitely places them outside the bounds of prose, and whether they can be received into those of verse does not concern us here.

General Comparison of Rhythms and Rhythmical Usages

In view of Professor Saintsbury's work, there is no necessity to attempt even a short sketch of the history of prose-rhythm, but no book such as this would be complete without a comparison between the rhythms of certain styles and authors which should provide some suggestive material, and which will at the same time point to a direction in which the student may usefully work.

From a rhythmical point of view three styles at least are markedly different. This statement does not deny the fact that no two authors write in exactly the same way, but asserts that there are at least three broad classes of rhythm within which the styles of different authors may, and do, vary enormously.

Although it cannot be said that the mastery of the

rhythm of prose has increased chronologically, in Anglo-Saxon times it was in its infancy. As was natural in an inflected language, the prevailing movement was trochaic and the tendency in prose was towards alliteration and rhythm in batches rather than to a continuous flow. A straightforward narrative style could be, and was, produced, but it was not until the fourteenth and fifteenth centuries that rhythm as we know it began to emerge. The influx of words from the Romance languages and from Latin was especially helpful in the making of "numerous" prose.

However, the simple manner of writing persisted and still persists, thus forming one of our three groups. As an early example of this type of writing the following passage may be quoted from Ascham's *Schoolmaster*:

In our forefather's time, when papistry, as a standing pool, covered and overflowed all England, few books were read in our tongue, saving certain books of chivalry, as they said for pastime and pleasure; which, as some say, were made in monasteries by idle monks or wanton canons. As one for example, Morte Arthur, the whole pleasure of which book standeth in two special points, in open man-slaughter and bold bawdry....

This is góod stúff | for wíse mén | to láugh at, | or hónest mén | to take pléasure at: | yet I knów, | when Gód's Bíble | was bánished | the Córt, | and Mórte Árthur | recéived | into the prínce's | chámber.[1]

These lines show something of the balance and alliteration which are well known features of Ascham's work.

[1] *The Schoolmaster*, p. 80 (Arber's English Reprints, London, 1897).

In many sentences balance is the only rhythmical feature, but sometimes, as in the sentence scanned above, the rhythm, though still owing much to balance, is tightened into a continuous thread. In this sentence there is a depth of feeling and a richness of sound which command admiration.

For the most part, however, balance is the only attempt at rhythmical effect to be found in the plain style. On account of their more modern language and syntax, the works of men like Jonson and Hobbes provide better examples of the plain style than do those of Ascham. Jonson's note on Shakespeare is known to many who have not read the fascinating collection in which it appears, and provides a good specimen of his style:

I remémber | the pláyers | have óften | méntioned it | as an hónor | to Shákespeare, | that in his wríting, | whatsoéver | he pénned, | he néver | blótted out | a líne. | My ánswer | hath béen, | "Wóuld he had blótted | a thóusand", | which they thóught | a malévolent | spéech. | I hád | not tóld | postérity this | but for théir ígnorance, | who chóse | thát círcumstance | to comménd | their fríend | by whereín | he móst | fáulted; | and to jústify | mine òwn : cándour, | for I lóved | the mán, | and do hónor | his mémory | on thís síde | idólatry | as múch | as ány. | He wás, | indéed, | hónest, | and of an ópen | and frée | náture; | had an éxcellent | fáncy, | bráve nótions, | and géntle | expréssions, | whereín | he flówed | with thàt facílity | that sómetimes | it was nécessary | he should be stópped.... But he redéemed | his víces | with his vírtues. | There was éver | móre in him | to be práised | than to be párdoned.[1]

[1] *Discoveries*, p. 23 (ed. F. E. Schelling, Boston, 1892).

The whole of *Discoveries* is of this "staccato" expression, a manner suited to, and largely caused by, the sententious nature of the matter, yet which is filed and smoothed so as to escape the charge of being merely jerky. Short feet of two or three syllables are prominent in this style.

The style of Hobbes is much more abrupt and less fluent than that of Jonson. His sentences, like Jonson's, are usually short, and so are his feet, but there is a crabbedness about his writing which makes his rhythms remarkable only in small sections instead of in longer periods. The following passage will serve for illustration:

To this warre of every man against every man, this also is consequent; that nothing can be Unjust. The notions of Right and Wrong, Justice and Injustice have there no place. Where there is no common Power, there is no Law: where no Law, no Injustice. Force, and Fraud, are in warre the two Cardinall vertues. Justice, and Injustice are none of the Faculties neither of the Body, nor Mind. If they were, they might be in a man that were alone in the world, as well as his Senses, and Passions.[1]

Although not of the same degree of rhythmical beauty, it is evident that this style is much more suitable for general purposes than elaborate "numerous" prose such as that of Browne or Taylor. Credit must therefore be given to those writers who, whilst practising this simple, straightforward way of writing, maintained it on the level of good prose as opposed to mere commonplace

[1] Hobbes, *Leviathan*, Part I, chap. xiii, p. 66 (Everyman's Library, London).

writing. It was inevitable that it should frequently descend to mere hackwork which has no claim to "style", but such lapses are the fault of the writers, not of the manner of writing.

One more example of this plain style, and that from Dryden, will suffice. The passage on Shakespeare is well known to students of Shakespearian criticism, but, as one of the "show-pieces" of Dryden's style, may be included here:

To begin then with Shakespeare. He was the man who of all modern and perhaps ancient poets had the largest and most comprehensive soul. All the images of nature were still present to him, and he drew them not laboriously but luckily: when he describes anything you more than see it, you feel it too. Those who accuse him to have wanted learning, give him the greater commendation: he was naturally learned; he needed not the spectacles of books to read nature; he looked inwards and found her there. I cannot say he is everywhere alike; were he so, I should do him injury to compare him with the greatest of mankind. He is many times flat, insipid; his comic wit degenerating into clenches, his serious swelling into bombast. But he is always great, when some great occasion is presented to him: no man can ever say he had a fit subject for his wit, and did not then raise himself as high above the rest of poets.

"Quantum lenta solent inter viburna cupressi".[1]

This is a good example of prose which is, at once, both conversational and literary. It possesses ease, grace, and fluency, but does not aim at elaborate rhythmical

[1] Dryden, *Essay of Dramatic Poesy* (*Essays*, ed. W. P. Ker, I, pp. 79–80, Oxford, 1900).

composition. It is eminently suited to writing of all kinds and can be practised with less difficulty and less danger than highly "numerous" prose.

Three very dissimilar examples of the "simple" style, varying from a rugged "crabbed" expression to fluency, ease, and polish, have been quoted, all of which, however, have in common a high percentage of short feet, and a simplicity of diction and syntactical arrangement which is less frequent in oratorical, or more elaborately rhythmed, prose. In none of the extracts is there any constant tendency for the prose to scan itself, but there are passages in which this tendency is marked, which are usually short, and which occur at irregular intervals. The staccato quality of the rugged style necessarily renders these passages short, whilst in the fluent style their shortness is caused by the numerous unaccented syllables and the consequent rapidity of pace, producing many sentences in which the contrast between strong and weak stress is but feebly heard and rhythmical tension, therefore, very low. Cadence is very infrequently heard, and is almost wholly confined to the bursts of "numerous" prose; interwoven cadence is rarer still.

Between this simple manner of writing and highly symphonic prose there lies a style which points to a conscious attempt at rhythmical elaboration of varying degrees, but which is antiphonic rather than symphonic in arrangement. In it, the elements of balance and antithesis, which are almost the only rhythmical devices of the simple style, are brought to the front and

developed into complicated systems. The best known
writer of this style is Johnson, who came upon it in his
efforts to elaborate and dignify the plain style. Other,
and very different, examples are to be found in Burke
and Gibbon, who also aimed at elaborate rhythmical
effects, but who, like Johnson, did not achieve the
variety in splendour of the great "numerous" prose of
the seventeenth and nineteenth centuries.

The prose of Johnson is always quoted as a good
(perhaps the best) example of balanced and antithetic
arrangement. Its frequently mechanically opposed
members drop out, as it were, and arrange themselves
in parallel alignments of their own accord. This feature
has been noticed above,[1] but, for the purpose of the
present comparison, another example may be given
here:

The task of an author is, either to teach what is not known,
or to recommend known truths by his manner of adorning them ;
either to let new light in upon the mind, and open new scenes to
the prospect, or to vary the dress and situation of common
objects, so as to give them fresh grace and more powerful attrac-
tions, to spread such flowers over the regions through which the
intellect has already made its progress, as may tempt it to
return, and take a second view of things hastily passed over, or
negligently regarded.[2]

Balance and antithesis are here almost the sole rhythmical
elements, and it would be an easy and pleasant exercise

[1] Chap. II, p. 69.

[2] Johnson, *The Rambler* (*English Prose Selections*, ed. Sir Hy.
Craik, IV, p. 141).

for the student to arrange this sentence in its corresponding groups as was done in a previous chapter.[1] The flow is much smoother than that of the harsher simple style as exemplified in Hobbes, but in comparison with the more graceful simple style as practised by Dryden it is not smoother, but rather slower and less limpid; its conscious rhythmical elaboration eliminates successions of weak, or feebly stressed, syllables, and causes attention to linger on the balanced periods. But, although rhythmical in large groups rather than in short ones, as was characteristic of the simple style, its rhythm, even in its most complex forms, is not continuous, but antiphonically arranged.

The rhythmical arrangement of Burke's prose is not so obvious as that of Johnson's, which shows a greater tendency to become mechanical. Burke's rhythmical range is extended by his delight in imagery which frequently results in his well-known "purple patches". The following paragraph is a good example of Burke's style:

Had it pléased | Gód | to contínue : to mè | the hópes | of succéssion, | I should have béen, | accórding | to my mediócrity, | and the mediócrity | of the áge | I líve in, | a sórt | of fóunder | of a fámily : | I should have léft | a són, | whó, | in áll | the póints | in whích | pérsonal | mérit | can be víewed, | in ˈscíence, | in èrudítion, | in génius, | in táste, | in hónour, | in gènerósity, | in humánity, | in évery | líberal | séntiment, | and évery | líberal | accómplishment, | wóuld not | have shówn himself | inférior | to the Dúke | of Bédford, | or to ány | of thóse | whom he tráces |

[1] Chap. ii, p. 69.

in his líne. | His Gráce | very sóon | would have wánted | áll | plàusibílity | in his attáck | upon thát | pássion | which belónged | móre | to míne | than to mé. | He would sóon | have supplíed | évery | defíciency, | and sýmmetrìzed | évery | dìspropórtion. | It wóuld not | have béen | for that succéssor | to resórt | to ány | stágnant | wásting | réservoir | of mérit | in mé, | or in ány | áncestry. | He hád | in himsélf | a sálient, | líving | spríng | of génerous | and mánly | áction. | Évery | dáy | he lived | he would have ré-púrchased | the bóunty | of the Crówn, | and tén tímes móre, | if tén tímes móre | he had recéived. | He was máde | a públic | créature ; | and had nó | enjóyment | whatéver | but in the perfórmance | of sóme | dúty. | At this éxigent | móment, | the lóss | of a fínished | mán | is not éasily | supplíed.[1]

Here, and everywhere throughout Burke's prose, the note of oratory is strong. The antiphonic manner is characteristic of nearly all oratorical prose. This passage, however, is much less prone to fall into mechanically opposed members than that quoted from Johnson. It lends itself more easily to continuous scansion, but tricks of phrase, akin to the balance of Johnson, can be discerned with little effort. One of the most prominent of these is the heaping-up of nouns, seen in,

in scíence, | in èrudítion, | in génius, | in táste, | in hónour, | in gènerósity, | in humánity, | in évery | líberal | séntiment, | and évery | líberal | accómplishment. ...

The rhythm of these, as the scansion will show, is skilfully varied, but even this cannot overcome the effect of artificiality.

[1] Burke, *Letter to a Noble Lord* (*Burke's Speeches*, ed. J. Burke, pp. 454-5, Dublin, 1865).

Another, but again different, example of the antiphonic style is to be found in the prose of Gibbon, of
which the following will serve as an example:

But his énemies | had pássed | the níght | in équal | disórder |
and anxíety. | The ìnconsíderate | cóurage | of Tórismund | was
témpted | to úrge | the pursúit, | tìll : he unexpéctedly | fóund
himself, | with a féw | fóllowers, | in the mídst | of the Scýthian |
wággons. | In the confúsion | of a noctúrnal | cómbat, | he was
thrówn | from his hórse; | and the Góthic | prínce | mùst have
pérished | like his fáther, | if his yóuthful | stréngth, | and the
intrépid | zéal | of his compánions, | had not réscued him | from
this dángerous | situátion. | In the sáme | mánner, | bùt on the
léft | of the líne, | Ætius | himsélf, | separáted | from his allíes, |
ígnorant | of their víctory, | and ánxious | for their fáte, |
encóuntered | and escáped | the hóstile | tróops | that were
scáttered | óver | the pláins | of Chálons ; | and at léngth | reached
the cámp | of the Góths, | whích he could ónly | fórtify | with a
slíght | rámpárt | of shíelds, | till the dáwn | of dáy. | The
impérial | géneral | was sóon | sátisfied | of the deféat | of
Áttila, | who stíll | remáined | ináctive | withín | his intrénch-
ments ; | and whén | he cóntempláted | the blóody | scéne, | he
obsérved, | with sécret | sàtisfáction, | that the lóss | had prínci-
pally | fállen | on the barbárians. | The bódy | of Theódoric, |
píerced | with hónourable | wóunds, | was discóvered | under a
héap | of the sláin : | his súbjects | bewáiled | the déath | of their
kíng | and fáther; | but their téars | were míngled | with sóngs |
and àcclamátions, | and his fúneral | rítes | were perfórmed | in
the fáce | of a vánquished | énemy.[1]

This is more pompous than the extract from the *Letter
to a Noble Lord* owing to the larger percentage of long

[1] Gibbon, *Decline and Fall of the Roman Empire.*

words which it contains. This in turn affects the length
of the feet, increasing the number containing four or
more syllables. The range of feet in this passage is also
rather greater than in that from Burke and it contains
a trick of using pairs of similar, or identical, feet, as
for example:

had not rescued him | from this dangerous,

and

in the confusion | of a nocturnal.

It is, however, in the larger rhythmical groups rather
than in individual feet that the chief differences
between the two passages are to be found. There are
here none of the enumerations which we noticed in
Burke, but there is, in places, an almost Johnsonian
swing, as, for instance, in:

In the same manner,
but on the left of the line,
  Ætius himself,
separated from his allies,
ignorant of their victory,
and anxious for their fate,
encountered
and escaped
  the hostile troops that were scattered over the plains of Châlons.

Usually, however, this swing is not too insistent and,
therefore, does not become so monotonous as that of
Johnson.

From a rhythmical point of view the best "numerous"
prose is symphonic or polyphonic, rather than anti-

phonic, in character; its harmonies are fully developed
and continuously arranged. In it full use is made of all
rhythmical devices and effects, but artifice does not
appear as it does even in the best examples of the
antiphonic style. This manner of writing flourished con-
spicuously in the seventeenth and nineteenth centuries.
In the former, besides the *Authorised Version of the
Bible*, the chief names are those of Browne and Taylor,
whilst in the latter there are such writers as De Quincey,
Ruskin, Swinburne, and Pater. Examples from four of
these authors will suffice, together with one from the
Authorised Version which may be quoted first:

> Though I **spéak** | **with the tóngues** | of *mén* | *and of Ángels,* |
> and **háve not** | **chárity,** | I am becóme | ,as sóunding | *bráss* |
> *or a tínkling* | *cýmbal.* | And thŏugh | I have the **gíft** | **of pró-**
> **phecy,** | and understánd | áll mýsteries | and áll knówledge: |
> and **thóugh** | **I have áll** ⁚ **fáith,** | so thàt ⁚ I could remóve |
> móuntains, | and have nó | chárity, | I am nóthing. | And thŏugh ⁚
> I bestów | àll my **góods** | **to féed** | **the póor,** | and though I
> gíve | my **bódy** | **to be búrned,** | and **háve not** | **chárity,** | it
> *prófiteth me* | *nóthing.*[1]

The temptation to quote the whole of this splendid
passage is great, but the student will know it already,
though he may not have criticised it from a rhythmical
point of view. The scansion should now speak for itself,
and it is intended to comment only on one or two
noteworthy adjustments. Variation of feet is skilfully
managed, but the most remarkable feature is the

---

[1] *Authorised Version of the Bible*, 1 Corinthians, chap. xiii, verses 1–3.

avoidance of monotony among those groups which are intended to correspond and which are very similar in form, as, for example, the following:

as sóunding | bráss,   or a tínkling | cýmbal

(here repetition is skilfully avoided by the use of the indefinite article and of nouns which differ in the number of syllables they contain);

áll mýsteries,   áll knówledge,   áll faíth

(in the same way careful adjustment is evident here);

and have not charity,   and have no charity, I am nothing,
and have not charity,   it profiteth me nothing

(these show that repetition of the same movement is not allowed even at distant intervals).

It has already been noticed[1] that this skilful variation of rhythm in enumerations and in synonymous phrases is an important feature of Biblical prose. Cadence is also noticeable here, but there are not many interwoven cadences.

The works of Jeremy Taylor are full of good things, but probably the finest example of his rhythm is that of the well-known passage on Prayer which Professor Saintsbury has scanned in detail in his *History of Prose Rhythm*[2] and part of which may be quoted here:

Práyer[3] | is the *péace* | *of our spírit,* | the **stíllness** | **of our** thóughts, | the *évenness* | *of rècolléction,* | the **séat** | **of mèditá-**

---

[1] See above, chap. II, p. 49.   [2] pp. 177 *et seq.*

[3] "Prayer" has been scanned throughout as a monosyllable. Professor Saintsbury hears it as a dissyllable, and the student will be able to choose for himself.

tion, | the rést | of our cáres | and the *cálm* | *of our témpest.* | *Práyer* | *is the issue* | of a quíet | mínd, | of untróubled | thóughts ; | it is the *dáughter* | *of chárity* | and the *síster* | *of méekness* ; | and hé | that práys | to Gód | with an ángry | —that is a tróubled | and discompósed— | spírit, | is like hím | that *retíres* | *into a báttle* | to mèditáte | and *séts up* | *his clóset* | in the óut*quárters* | *of an ármy* | and chóoses | a *fróntier* | *gárrison* | to be wíse in. | Ánger | is a *pérfect* | *áliendtion* | of the mínd | from práyer, | and *thérefore* | *is cóntrary* | to that atténtion | which presénts | our práyers | in a ríght | líne | to Gód. | For só | have I séen | a lárk | rísing | from his béd | of gráss, | sóaring | úpwards | and *sínging* | *as he ríses* | and hópes | to gét | to Héaven | and clímb | abóve | the clóuds ; | but the póor bírd | was béaten báck | with the lóud | síghings | of an éastern | wínd | and his *mótion* | *made irrégular* | and incónstant, | descénding | móre | at évery *bréath* | *of the témpest* | than it cóuld | recóver | by the vìbrátion | *and fréquent* | **wéighing** | of his wíngs ; | till the líttle | créature | was fórced | to sit dówn | and pánt | and *stáy* | *till the stórm* | *was óver* ; | and thén | it máde | a prósperous | flíght | and did ríse | and síng | as if it had léarned | *músic* | *and mótion* | *from an ángel* | as he pássed | sòmetímes | through the áir | about his **ministries** | hére | belów.[1]

Not the least noticeable feature of this, and the following, passages is the inevitability of their scansion. There is little, or no, difficulty in marking the feet, and cadences pervade the whole. Interwoven cadences of all types are common here, adding not a little to the undulation of the rhythm and complicating its harmonies.

[1] Cadences of the same kind overlap as follows : "rises and hópes", 4–1, and "hópes to gét to Héaven", 6–4–2 ; "músic and mótion", *planus*, and "mótion from an ángel", extension of *planus*.

The rhythmical correspondence of these phrases in the first sentence shows careful adjustment:

péace of our spírit	′× ×′×
stíllness of our thóughts	′× × ×′
évenness of rècolléction	′× × ×ˌ×′×
séat of mèditátion	′×ˌ×′×
rést of our cáres	′× ×′
cálm of our témpest	′× ×′×

The phrase "of untroubled thoughts" is skilfully bound to "issue" by possessing identically the same rhythmical movement as "of a quiet mind". The simile of the lark is famous, and, for beauty of rhythm, may be ranked among the finest "numerous" sentences in English Literature. The close correspondence of rhythm and sense shows the hand of a master. Professor Saintsbury comments[1] on the way in which metrical movements are suggested throughout but only appear very occasionally, and even then only in short bursts, and are never allowed to predominate. This effect is largely due to the pervasive character of the cadences which sweeten and order the rhythm considerably.

Passages such as this provide material for almost endless comments, but space forbids, and it is intended here to indicate only those features which may not appear immediately from the scansion.

The next example will be taken from Sir Thomas

[1] *History of Prose Rhythm*, p. 181.

Browne who is perhaps the greatest master of English "numerous" prose:

Nów : sínce : thése : déad : bónes | have alréady | óut-lásted | the líving ones | of Methúselàh, | and in a yárd | **under** **gróund,** | and **thín** | **wálls** | **of cláy,** | óut-wórn | all the **stróng** | **and spécious** | *búildings* | *abóve it*; | and *quíetly* | *résted* | ùnder the drúms | and trámplings | of thrée | cónquèsts; | what Prínce | can prómise | súch | diútúrnity | ùnto his rélicks, | or **míght** **not** | **gládly** | **sáy,**

"Sic ego componi versus in ossa velim ".

Tíme, | which ántiquàtes | Àntíquities | and hath an árt | to máke dúst | of áll thíngs, | hàth yét spáred | thèse mínor | mónuments.

This is the opening paragraph of the famous Chapter 5 of *Hydriotaphia*, a chapter which is, perhaps, the longest example in English of sustained prose harmony of the highest order, and which Professor Saintsbury justly calls "an unbroken, and, at most, spaced and rested symphony".[1] Owing to the prevalence of strong stresses here, cadence is not so frequent as in the passage quoted from Jeremy Taylor, but the rhythm is not less beautiful and shows careful adjustment. Jeremy Taylor's gentle strains have been replaced by the voluminous harmonies of an organ or full orchestra. The opening has been scanned in several ways,[2] the chief of which are, perhaps, (1) as five monosyllables,

---

[1] *History of Prose Rhythm*, p. 183.
[2] See above, chap. II, p. 39.

and (2) as monosyllable, iamb, spondee, ´|×´|´´. In
"unto his relicks" there is a marked tendency to form
a *cursus planus* by setting up an accent on the first
syllable of "unto", a tendency which is strengthened
by the ability of such words as "unto", "into", etc., to
take a strong stress on either or neither syllable.[1]

Perhaps Browne's finest sentence, from a rhythmical
point of view, is the following:

But *mán | is a nóble | ánimal, | spléndid | in áshes, |* and
pómpous | in the gráve, | sólem*nízing | natívities | and* **déaths |**
with équal | lústre, | nor omítting | céremonies | of brávery | in
the ínfamy| of his náture.[2]

This is an excellent example of a highly cadenced and
intricately rhythmed sentence, and shows Browne's
extraordinary felicity in composing phrases which are
at once unexpected in their associations and beautiful
in their harmony.

De Quincey provides a sentence which Professor
Saintsbury considers to be one of the finest examples
of rhythmed prose, and which he quotes and comments
upon in some detail.[3] The extract which will be con-

[1] See P. Fijn van Draat, *Rhythm in English Prose.*
[2] Sir T. Browne, *Hydriotaphia*, chap. v.
Two native cadences overlap:

"-tívities and déaths ", 5–1,
"déaths with équal lústre", 6–4–2.

The correspondence of "céremonies of brávery" and "ínfamy of
his náture" is noteworthy. Both approximate to forms of the *cursus.*
[3] *History of Prose Rhythm*, pp. 307, 308.

sidered here is from the well-known description of Our
Lady of Darkness:

But the thírd | síster, | who is *álso* | *the yóungest*! |—Húsh! |
whísper | **while we tálk** | **of hér**! | Hér **kíngdom** | **ís not** |
lárge, | or élse | **nó flésh could líve;** | but withín | that kíng-
dom | áll **pówer** | **is hérs.** | Her héad, | túrreted | like **thát** | **of**
Cýbelé, | ríses | **álmost** | **beyónd** | **the réach** | **of síght.** | Shè
dróops not; | and her éyes, | **rísing** | **so hígh,** | might be *hídden* |
by dístance. | But **béing what they áre,** | they *cánnot* | *be hídden;* |
through the **tréble** | **véil** | **of crápe** | **that she wéars,** | the
fíerce | *líght* | *of a blázing* | *mísery* | that *résts not* | *for mátins* |
or véspers, | for nóon | of dáy | or nóon | of níght, | for **ébbing** |
or for flówing | **tíde,** | may be **réad** | **from the véry** | **gróund.**[1]

Cadences are common, both overlapping and single,
and are carefully handled. The sequence

for nóon | of dáy | or nóon | of níght

is a little too regular but regularity in the next sequence
is skilfully avoided by the repetition of "for":

for ébbing | or for flówing | tíde.

De Quincey frequently shows a liking for groups of
similar, or even the same, feet, and in so doing occasionally drops into metrical, or quasi-metrical, movement. In
some parts of his work, rhythm bears a marked resemblance to that of Browne.

The last example of the symphonic style, and one

[1] De Quincey, *Suspiria de Profundis.*

Native cadences overlap: "álmost beyónd", 4–1, and "-yónd the
réach of síght", 5–3–1, "tréble véil of crápe", 5–3–1, and "crápe that
she wéars", 4–1. *Cursus* overlap: "résts not for mátins", *planus,* and
"mátins or véspers", *planus.*

with which this book must close, is taken from Landor and is quoted by Professor Saintsbury as "unsurpassed since the renaissance of numerous prose".[1] For this reason alone its re-inclusion here will be justified, and further secrets of its harmony may be shown by scanning for cadence as well as for prose-rhythm:

There is a glóom | in déep lóve | as in déep | wáter; | there is a sílence in it | which suspénds | the fóot, | and the fólded | árms | and the dejécted | héad | are the ímages | it reflécts. | Nó vóice | shákes | its súrface; | the *Múses* | *themsélves* | *appróach it* | with a tárdy | and a tímid | stép, | and with a lów | and trémulous | and mélancholy | sóng.[2]

Variety is prominent, but cadence is not so pervasive as in the preceding example, and the rhythm is, therefore, simpler. The words are short, in apt accordance with the limpidity and calmness of the atmosphere. Two phrases,

and the fólded | árms,   × ×ˊ×ˊ,

and

and the dejécted | héad,   × × ×ˊ×ˊ,

are very similar but do not disturb the continuity of the movement. This untroubled flow of harmony is an essential ingredient of the best rhythmical prose. Balance, however finely developed, very quickly tends to become monotonous, and cannot be as satisfying as the continuous movement of the symphonic or polyphonic style.

[1] *History of Prose Rhythm*, p. 339.
[2] Native cadences overlap: "glóom in déep lóve", 4-2-1, and "lóve as in déep wáter", 6-3-2.

It would have been possible to have multiplied almost indefinitely the examples quoted above, but such a "sylva" of passages of rhythmical prose has no place here, and has partly, though to a certain extent unintentionally, been accomplished in Professor Cowl's *Anthology of Imaginative Prose.* Comments on the selected passages could also have been increased enormously, but at this stage the scansion should speak for itself, and the student should have no difficulty in appreciating the fundamental differences between the three chief types of rhythmical prose. For other chosen examples of English prose, reference may be made to Sir Henry Craik's *English Prose Selections,* and for the study of prose-rhythm from an historical standpoint Professor Saintsbury's *History of Prose Rhythm* will prove to be indispensable.

GLOSSARY

Advance and recession of strong stress (*v.* p. 59).

Advance of strong stress occurs in a succession of feet when the strongly stressed syllable advances towards the beginning of the foot in each consecutive foot. The type is: × × ×ʹ | × ×ʹ× | ×ʹ× × | ʹ× × ×.

The opposite to this is recession of strong stress, where the strongly stressed syllable recedes towards the end of the foot in each successive foot. The type is: ʹ× × × | ×ʹ× × | × ×ʹ× | × × ×ʹ.

Antiphonic, symphonic and continuous rhythms.

"Antiphonic" is the adjective used to describe rhythm which is built up of carefully balanced rhythmical groups. It is to be noticed chiefly in oratorical or rhetorical prose (*v.* chap. ɪᴠ). As their names imply, "continuous" and "symphonic" rhythms are the opposite of the antiphonic movement, as these rhythms are woven into a continuous thread.

Cadence (*v.* chap. ɪɪɪ).

This is the name for certain rhythmical sequences which occur frequently throughout numerous prose, and especially at emphatic places, and are used, either consciously or unconsciously, because they appear to be more effective than others. In highly rhythmical prose they occur with such frequency that they often overlap. All cadences begin on a strongly stressed syllable and contain both strong and weak syllables. They have this in common with metre that they may cut across words, that is,

they need not begin with the beginning or end with the end of
a word. There are two kinds of cadences:

1. Those which may be regarded as equivalent to the classical
   cursus and their extensions, and which may be grouped
   under the name *cursus*. There are three chief forms of the
   cursus, all of which end on a light syllable.
   (a) *planus:*   ′××′×,   5–2.
       Extension: ′×××′×,   6–2.
   (b) *tardus:*   ′××′××,   6–3.
       Extension: ′×××′××,   7–3.
   (c) *velox:*   ′××′×′×,   7–4–2.
       Extension: ′×××′×′×, 8–4–2.

2. Those which do not conform to any type of the *cursus* and
   may, therefore, be called *native*. There are many varieties
   of *native* cadence, ending with either strong or weak
   syllables (*v.* pp. 83 *et seq.*). The most common native cadences
   are ′××′, 4–1, and ′×××′, 5–1.

Cursus.

The ancient writers of Greece and Rome aimed at special
rhythmical effects at the ends of the different parts of their
sentences. For this purpose certain rhythmical sequences were
favoured, and these they called *cursus*, the name implying "a run",
thus suiting the trochaic movement which was an essential part
of their composition (*v.* pp. 74 *et seq.*). There were three chief
types of *cursus* which have been noticed above under "Cadence".

Foot.

There is still much controversy and disagreement among
prosodists as to what is, and what constitutes, a foot in metre.
For the purpose of prose-rhythm, however, the term may be
explained as follows:

In any logical sequence of speech sounds the terms tend to arrange themselves in groups, and a more definite separation is noticed between the groups than between the individual sounds composing a group. In analysis these groups are called "feet". As a rule, in every foot, there is at least one strongly stressed syllable around which the other syllables tend to group themselves. A foot may contain as many as three strong stresses, but more than three tend to split up into two or more feet. Five may be regarded as the maximum number of syllables which, under ordinary circumstances, may combine to form a foot. In less rhythmical prose, groups of six, or even seven, syllables occasionally assume the position of feet but such groups are comparatively rare in "numerous" prose. Every foot begins with the beginning and ends with the end of a word, but may contain more than one word (*v.* pp. 19–20, 35). Thus, in prose-rhythm, foot-divisions never cut words as they do in metre.

Gradation.

A gradual increase or decrease in the number of syllables in successive feet, Professor Saintsbury terms "gradation" (*v.* pp. 53–5). Gradation downwards, from many syllables to few, is particularly common at the ends of sentences.

Long and short.

When these terms are used for syllabic values, they refer to the time taken to pronounce, or, in other words, the "duration" of, those syllables. The "duration" of any syllable may be said to be the amount of time occupied by that syllable (*v.* pp. 4, 5, 8).

Pitch or tone.

The "pitch" or "tone" of any syllable is the position in the musical scale occupied by the sound of that syllable.

Prose-rhythm.

This term is used here to denote the grouping of syllables into feet whose stresses are logical as opposed to metrical in verse (*v.* p. 104). In the scansion of prose-rhythm, therefore, foot-divisions never cut the words. Each foot is made up of one or more words, grouped according to sense. *Prose-rhythm should not be confused with the rhythm of prose which is made up of both prose-rhythm and cadence.*

Quantivists.

This is the name given to those theorists who believe that speech-rhythm is based on the relationship of syllabic quantities, that is, that the time durations of certain syllables are long, and of others short, by nature or position, and that, although stress may be superimposed, English verse is primarily based on a regular recurrence and pattern formation of these quantities (*v.* p. 4).

Recurrence (*v.* pp. 13–16).

Recurrence is necessary to all forms of rhythm, though it is not so marked in prose as it is in poetry. In "numerous", or rhythmical, prose there is recurrence at longer and more irregular intervals than in poetry; in poetry recurrence is so insistent as to set up a base or "norm".

Recurrence in prose appears in many forms, the chief of which are:

(*a*) gradation of prose-feet;

(*b*) cadences, both single and interwoven;

(*c*) balancing of cadences, of members of a sentence, or of the sentences themselves, the two latter being particularly common in rhetorical prose (*v.* p. 15).

GLOSSARY 135

Rhythm (*v.* chap. I).

Rhythm in general is the organisation of perceptions in an orderly way by the mind (*v.* p. 2), but, in this book, the term is used to refer to auditory rhythm, which may be defined as the organisation of sound stimulated in the mind by the repetition of a series of auditory events in time. Rhythm in English speech is primarily determined by stress.

Rhythm, kinds of (*v.* pp. 20–1).

The different types of rhythm may be grouped into four classes:

1. *Rising rhythm* is that in which each foot begins with one or more weakly stressed syllables and rises to one or more strongly stressed syllables. (e.g. iamb, anapaest, anti-bacchius, "ionic a minore", etc.).

2. *Falling rhythm* is that in which each foot begins with one or more strongly stressed syllables and ends with one or more weakly stressed syllables (e.g. trochee, dactyl, bacchius, etc.).

3. *Level rhythm* is that in which each foot is wholly made up of strong stresses[1] (e.g. monosyllable, spondee, etc.).

4. *Waved rhythm* in which each foot begins and ends on the same kind of stress, and contains both strong and weak stresses (e.g. amphibrach, 2nd and 3rd paeons, antispast, etc.).

Rising and *waved* rhythms are the most common measures in English speech; *falling* and *level* rhythms are comparatively rare.

[1] The existence of the "pyrrhic", × ×, is doubtful, that of the "tribrach", × × ×, and "proceleusmatic", × × × ×, is even more doubtful (*v.* p. 23).

Rhythmical material.

Rhythmical material is that which stimulates a rhythmical organisation or response in the mind (*v.* p. 7).

Stress, accent, weight.

Stress has been defined by Professor Abercrombie as denoting the "force of breath-impulse initiating syllables". *Accent* denotes the resultant of the combination of both *pitch* and *stress*, but, since an increase in *stress* usually produces a higher *pitch*, *accent* is frequently used as being synonymous with *stress*. Another alternative in common use is *weight*. Accentual rhythm is one which is primarily based upon stress.

Stress, kinds of.

The different degrees of stress may be grouped broadly into three classes:

(a) *Strong stress* denoted in scansion by "´". Syllables which require the greatest force of breath-impulse, or, in other words, which bear the greatest emphasis, are said to be strongly stressed (*v.* p. 17).

(b) *Weak stress* denoted in scansion by "×" when the rhythm is quoted without the text. When the text is quoted, weak syllables are left unmarked. This is the opposite of strong stress; weakly stressed syllables do not bear emphasis.

(c) *Secondary stress* denoted in scansion by "ˋ". This occupies an intermediate position between strong and weak stress. It is distinctly heavier than the latter, but lighter than the former. It is frequently set up in sequences of three or more light syllables (*v.* pp. 17–18).

BIBLIOGRAPHY

Guest, E. *History of English Rhythms*. London, 1838.

Clark, A. C. In *Classical Review*, xix, pp. 164–72. 1905.

Omond, T. S. *English Metrists* (18th and 19th Centuries). Oxford, 1907.

Clark, A. C. *Fontes Prosae Numerosae*. Oxford, 1909.
—— *The Cursus in Mediaeval and Vulgar Latin*. Oxford, 1910.

Fijn van Draat, P. *Rhythm in English Prose*. Heidelberg, 1910.

Saintsbury, G. *A History of English Prose Rhythm*. London, 1912.

Shelly, J. "Rhythmical Prose in Latin and English", in *Church Quarterly Review*, April 1912.

Clark, A. C. *Prose Rhythm in English*. Oxford, 1913.

MacColl, D. S. "Rhythm in English Verse, Prose, and Speech", in *Essays and Studies of the English Association*, v. Oxford, 1914.

Patterson, W. M. *The Rhythm of Prose*. Columbia Univ. Press, New York, 1917.

Croll, M. W. "The Cadence of English Oratorical Prose", in *Studies in Philology*, Univ. of N. Carolina, Jan. 1919.

Omond, T. S. *English Metrists*. Oxford, 1921.

Elton, O. "English Prose Numbers", in *A Sheaf of Papers*. Liverpool U.P., 1922. (First published in *Essays and Studies of the English Association*, iv. Oxford, 1913.)

Abercrombie, L. *Principles of English Prosody, Part I*. London, 1923.

Smith, E. *The Principles of English Metre*. Oxford, 1923.

Sonnenschein, E. A. *What is Rhythm?* Oxford, 1925.

Novotný, F. *État Actuel des Études sur le Rhythme de la Prose Latine.* Lwów, 1929.

Craik, Sir Hy. *English Prose Selections* (5 vols.). London, 1890–6.

Cowl, R. P. *Anthology of English Imaginative Prose.* London undated.

For EU product safety concerns, contact us at Calle de José Abascal, 56–1°,
28003 Madrid, Spain or eugpsr@cambridge.org.